CRE▲TIVE
HOMEOWNER®

FOURTH EDITION

DECK
Designs

Great Ideas from Top Deck Designers

STEVE CORY

CREATIVE HOMEOWNER®

690.893
COR

Copyright © 2015

CRE🏠TIVE
HOMEOWNER®

Creative Homeowner® is a registered trademark of New Design Originals Corporation.

Deck Designs, Fourth Edition
Acquisition Editor: Ray Wolf
Copy Editor: Katie Weeber
Cover and Page Designer: Jason Deller
Editor: Timothy O. Bakke, Sr.

Printed in Singapore

Current Printing (last digit)
10 9 8 7 6 5 4 3 2 1

ISBN 978-1-58011-716-6

Creative Homeowner, *www.creativehomeowner.com*, is an imprint of New Design Originals Corporation and distributed exclusively by Fox Chapel Publishing Company, Inc., 800-457-9112, 1970 Broad Street, East Petersburg, PA 17520.

CONTENTS

INTRODUCTION 6
WHY A DECK? 6
HOW THE BOOK WORKS 8

PART ONE **DESIGNING YOUR DECK** 10

HOW TO DESIGN 10
SIZE AND SHAPE 12
EASY ON THE EYES 13
DECK AND LANDSCAPE 17
SUN, WIND, AND RAIN 17
THE OUTDOOR ROOMS APPROACH 18
DINING AND ENTERTAINING OPTIONS 20
CEILINGS AND WALLS 21
LIGHTING OPTIONS 22
GARDENING 22
HOW IT IS PUT TOGETHER 23
STRUCTURAL AND VISIBLE MATERIALS 27

PART TWO **MEET THE BUILDERS** 30

UNIQUE DECK BUILDERS 34
JOEL BOYER

THE OVERALL DESIGN 36
FINISH MATERIALS 37
Split-Level with Wood Bar and Spa 40
Cozy Retreat 46
Spacious Rooftop Getaway 52
Versatile Family Room 56
Private City Loft 60

DECKS, INC. 66
IVAN ARANA

HIS DESIGNS 68
FINISH MATERIALS 68
CRAFTSMANSHIP 71
Well Rounded 74
Expansive Balcony 86

Beautiful Symmetry 94
Woodsy Retreat 98
Woody Gem 104

BARRETT OUTDOORS 108
GUSTAVO "GUS" DE LA CRUZ

DESIGNING AROUND THE FURNITURE 110
DESIGNS THAT POP 110
OUTDOOR KITCHENS AND LIGHTING 113
DECKING AND RAILING MATERIALS 113

Jewel by the Pool 116
Curvy Party Deck 124
Relaxation Station 132
Zigzag Charm 136
Half Circle with Wings 142

ROLLING RIDGE DECK AND OUTDOOR LIVING 146
BARRY STREETT

THE DESIGN PROCESS 148
OUTDOOR KITCHENS AND FIREPLACES 148
RAILINGS AND CURVES 151

Log Cabin Chic 154
Curved This Way, Then That 160
Scallops and Curves 164
Private Family Room 170
Rocky Mountain High Life 176

CLOUGH CONSTRUCTION 182
SCOTT AND DEANNE CLOUGH

DESIGN APPROACHES 184
ENGINEERING FOR STRENGTH 186

Natural Jewel 190
Sunset Setting 198
Movie Star Setting 204
Open Nest among the Trees 212

RESOURCE GUIDE 216
PHOTO CREDITS 219
GLOSSARY 220
METRIC EQUIVALENTS 221
INDEX 222
SAFETY 224

Introduction

A well-designed, sturdily built deck is an upgrade with plenty of perks. It can:

- Comfortably extend your indoor living space and make you want to spend more time outdoors, providing a pleasant place to get away from it all to relax or read under swaying branches.

- Take you out of the kitchen to prepare meals, whether on a simple outdoor grill or a full-scale outdoor kitchen.

- Expand your entertaining space, providing extra room to accommodate guests. Its natural ambiance makes it an inviting setting for convivial parties as well as intimate gatherings. Moving some or all of the mess outside lifts a burden from the hosts and makes gatherings more relaxing.

On a carefully designed deck, you will step naturally from inside the house to the deck surface, and you will move easily from one area to the next, guided subconsciously by invisible pathways. You will never feel cramped when cooking, dining, or relaxing, and your view of the backyard will be enhanced rather than obscured by railings and the orientation of the deck. Getting the design right will meet your expectations and will likely surprise you with unanticipated pleasures as your repertoire of outdoor activities grows.

Whether you plan to hire a professional contractor or build it yourself, this book can be your guide. Here you will find a wealth of ideas—both general and specific—for dreaming as well as practical building. This is the fourth all-new edition of *Deck Designs*. Previous editions have sold close to half a million copies and have helped many homeowners choose and achieve the deck of their dreams. This new edition extends that tradition of excellence; we seek to retain the successful features of the past while showing all new ideas by some great new builders.

Why a Deck?

Let's start by asking a fundamental question: Why do you want a deck? How will it improve your life? Here are some possibilities:

MONEY. Real estate experts say dollars invested in a deck increase the value of your house and improve its curb appeal. Adding a nice deck will give you a near-100-percent return in value, meaning for every dollar you put in, your home's value will go up nearly the same amount.

R AND R. An inviting deck will get you out of the house so you can enjoy some fresh air. Life seems to be less hectic outdoors, and meals are more casual. While you hang out on your deck, you can enjoy nature, appreciate your yard's special features, and perhaps cultivate herbs for your family dinner.

GOOD EATS. Everything tastes better when cooked and eaten outdoors. If you incorporate an outdoor kitchen in the deck's design—or at least provide ample space for a grill and side table—you may find yourself exploring new recipes and finding renewed enjoyment cooking old favorites. You may also be inclined to host special events more often.

PARTY HEARTY. Entertaining is more relaxed on a deck. You don't have to worry about the mess, and you have additional space for guests to hang out. Food hot off the grill has a fun factor—creative efforts like grilled s'mores or jalapeno poppers add sparkle to a menu. Lights artfully strung overhead make an evening gathering memorable. A deck lets you simplify the game plan and still get excellent results.

FAMILY CIRCLE. A well-built deck is a great place for kids to hang out, and many families add kid-friendly touches like a sandbox, a water table, a toy crate, or kid-sized furniture. It gets young people away from the TV or computer, and when they have friends over—to play or for a birthday party—they can indulge in messy activities that would wreak havoc inside the house.

Family entertainment center.
This wide deck uses railing design and furniture placement to define distinct zones for relaxing with a book, dining, and enjoying a drink or snack at the bar.

How the Book Works

The first part of the book, "Designing Your Deck," is built around a gallery of decks from around the country. But it's more than just a bunch of pretty pictures. The photos illustrate the points of the accompanying text and walk you through the design process. You'll learn how to dream up a deck that looks fabulous and is customized for your uses.

You will also find a crash course in deck building—not full instructions, but enough information to make you an educated consumer. You will learn how decks are constructed, as well as some of the major variations due to sites, designs, and building codes.

The rest of the book features decks from five of the USA's best designer-builders. These builders employ time-tested methods and materials suitable for a variety of deck types and building codes. You will find a profile of each builder that summarizes his design approach and building methods, along with a gallery of his work.

For each builder there will be five or six feature decks. For each deck, you will see a section called "The Design," discussing the deck's shape, size, and materials, and why it was designed the way it was. Then in a section called "Building the Deck," you will learn how the deck was constructed—not complete step-by-step directions, but overall approaches accompanied by a closer look at various distinctive portions of the deck.

The featured decks in this book have actually been built, and most of them have been tested for at least several years in the real world, so you know they are durable. As the writer/photographer, I have visited almost all of these decks, and I have often heard homeowners rave about them. All of these decks are loved.

Relaxing water view. Built low to the ground, this deck gets away without railings, which would detract from the awesome surroundings. The perimeter benches perform double duty: providing seating and preventing guests from stepping off the deck.

USING THIS BOOK

I can't emphasize enough that this is a book to help you imagine and dream—not a manual for deck construction. It aims to get your creative juices flowing and provide a palette of ideas, both general and specific. Good ideas are sprinkled throughout, so I suggest that you browse through the entire book rather than zero in on just one or two designs.

Houses and backyards are individual, so a deck plan should be just as individual. Even if you find a single deck that is "exactly what you want," you will probably need to modify it at least a little. More likely, you will find several decks that have elements that you would like to incorporate into your own plan. You may, for instance, choose to mix and match the railing style from one deck and the kind of decking from another.

Building codes for decks have gotten significantly more stringent over the past ten years or so. And these codes vary greatly from locale to locale; even adjacent towns may have vastly different codes. Your deck must conform to these local codes in many specific ways, such as how framing attaches to the house via a ledger board; the size and spacing of framing members; railing construction and height; and many other considerations. This book will help you understand most of those issues.

Before you get into all of the grimy details, however, settle down into a comfortable chair or hammock, perhaps with a significant other, and enjoy this book. After all, a deck is essentially a play area for adults, so every great deck starts with some wishing and dreaming.

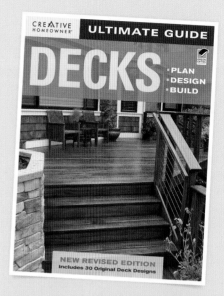

Building Your Own Deck? If you plan to build a deck yourself, also pick up Creative Homeowner's *Ultimate Guide: Decks: Plan, Design, Build (fourth edition)*. It presents detailed step-by-step instructions for all aspects of deck building. It also includes additional deck designs. If, however, you intend to hire a contractor to build your deck, the book you are holding in your hand can certainly stand on its own.

Conforming deck. Make sure your new deck conforms to local building codes by working with your town's building department. Codes will cover aspects such as foundations, stairs (rise and run), size of beams, railings, and the like.

PART ONE:
Designing Your Deck

The next thirty pages tell how to make a fresh design for your deck, from the basic style and contours, to the materials for decking and railing, to the little details, amenities, and furnishings.

How to Design

You could simply hire a deck designer/builder, or even an architect, to design a deck for you. But do not be afraid to jump into the design process—it will make the deck feel more your own. Even a few hours spent thinking seriously about your deck can ensure against design mistakes and allow you to inject features that will give your deck a personality that suits you.

You probably do not have much design experience. But compared with a house (or even a kitchen) a deck is a pretty simple and straightforward project. You have no doubt seen a good number of decks, and you are a reasonably creative person, right? With a little imagination and some drawing tools, you will be able to envision it pretty completely. Also, your house and yard will likely go a long way toward determining the deck's shape and size. So don't be afraid to jump in; designing can be fun and rewarding.

A LITTLE LARCENY. Do as all great writers, artists, and architects do: Start by stealing some ideas. Do not worry that your deck will end up looking just like someone else's: Your house and yard will make it look different, and even a couple of changes—decking material or railing style, for instance—can make even a copycat deck appear distinctive.

Embark on your "life of crime" by grabbing ideas from this book. Also, ask friends and neighbors about their decks. Most people—even strangers—will be happy to talk about what they love and what they would change. It is not unusual for people who love their deck to recommend one or two things that they would do differently if they had

the chance; these mistakes can usually be avoided in the planning stage, but will be hard to fix once the deck is built.

GATHER THE TROOPS. Have a little family meeting, perhaps on the site where the deck will be, and learn what your spouse and kids would like the new deck to do for them. There will be practical considerations, such as a clear pathway to the garbage, or deck and railing surfaces that are easy to keep clean. Some people may want to engage in activities like container gardening. Some may want solitude; others may want a good space for parties. Some may like the yard so much that they prefer a small deck to a large one.

DRAW AND REDRAW. Software programs for designing decks have proliferated in recent years, but may be difficult to use and expensive. By making a series of rough sketches, you can think through the basic contours of your deck and how it will work. (If you try to do this in front of a computer, you may miss the nuances and character of your space.) Some suggestions for creating initial drawings: try taking overhead photos of the space from a ladder, making several copies, and penciling in deck contours. Or draw on graph paper to get everything to scale. Hang your favorite designs on the refrigerator, and let everyone think about and discuss them for a few weeks. You will end up discarding many of your attempts, but you will gradually develop a plan that will work for your home and your family.

Comfortable retreat. It may take a little effort (and family collaboration) to design your deck, but benefits will outweigh the trials once you have a lovely spot like this to relax with the family.

Size and Shape

Consider the overall contours of the deck to be sure it will feel comfortable next to the house and within the landscape—and so it will meet your needs.

SIZE. A deck should not be so large as to make the house look small, nor should it look like a midget appendage.

To size the deck for family activities, think about your home's living room to gauge how much space is needed for comfortably hanging out. One common mistake is to make a deck too narrow. To accommodate both seating and a traffic path, a deck's depth should be at least 7 feet (2.1m), and preferably wider. Another common mistake is to make a deck so large that it creates an awkward situation in the yard—for instance, you have to go up and down the deck stairs to get from one side of the yard to the other.

Browse furniture while you are planning to be sure you will have space for a table, chairs, and a path around the table and chairs. Even a modest size table usually requires a 12-foot (3.7m) square area. That means that a bargain-priced 10 x 10-foot (3m x 3m) deck will probably be frustrating. Other use areas—cooking, sunning, play space, hot tub—also need traffic paths. Think carefully about where your deck stairs will go; it should be easy for people

to get from the house to the stairs without interfering with the chef or diners, and the stairs should lead to a good place in the yard.

SHAPE. The shape of your outdoor space and the back of the house will help determine the best shape for your deck. A good design will feel at home in the space and call attention to the advantages of the yard. While a simple rectangular deck works well in some situations and may be a good starting point, consider adding definition to use areas with curves, tiers, geometric angles, or bump-out sections. For instance, a bump-out for a grill gives the chef a separate cooking space that does not interfere with traffic patterns on the rest of the deck.

Many houses have a straight or near-straight rear wall, and a deck design with some complexity can feel less tacked on and more interesting. The addition of curves or angles, especially when complemented by judicious landscaping, can attractively soften the add-on effect and give you a unique design that works for the space and your family's needs. If your house exterior is formal and stately, on the other hand, too many curves and angles can look out of place.

Curvy showpiece. This deck could have been a typical add-on, but the materials, curved perimeter, and inlaid star in the main part of the deck add up to make it a stunner.

Easy on the Eyes

Once you have established basic contours for your deck, envision how it will look. Some considerations:

COLOR. Your deck will introduce new colors to the palette in your yard, and these colors will occupy one-third or more of the overall back-of-the-house view. The way the color of the finished product will look can be difficult to visually gauge, even with software, and the appearance will be different in direct sunlight versus the shade. Before you choose, take boards home to see how they look from a distance against the house.

If your home's exterior is brick, most wood or composite materials will be a pleasing complement. But if your home is painted or has vinyl siding, take your time choosing decking materials. A home exterior that is painted a grayish putty color, for instance, may clash with decking materials that have reddish stain tones, especially if the two colors are the same intensity. It may be preferable to choose colors in the same family. Railings, fascia, and skirting often look better in a different color or material from the decking.

Complementary colors. The white railing on this deck echoes the white house trim. The cedar decking, with its reddish-yellow hue, would clash with house siding that had cool tones in its color.

Classy deck. The soft gray tones of the decking boards on this large deck blend well with the white siding, giving the whole setting a classic look.

Continuity. The design and coloring of the pergola framing members, the railing posts, and the support posts are all of a piece, giving the deck a uniformly classic appearance.

Points of interest. Coming out of the house, the "Z" benches are an effective focal point on this geometric, symmetrical deck. Approaching the deck, the home's chimney, centered within the deck structure, is the focal point.

THEME AND VARIATION. A good design often has a theme that repeats itself in a couple of different places to add unity and appeal. A curved or angled section may occur in two places, for instance, once in a bigger section and once in a smaller section. Or the railing design may echo the design or color of the fascia, skirting, or house trim. If your design includes a large octagonal or circular bump-out for a dining area, consider adding a smaller bump-out in the same shape at the other end, perhaps for a grill or reading spot.

FOCAL POINTS. A focal point is an area of distinction—a view from the deck or a feature like a fire pit to enjoy on the deck itself—that sets a deck apart from others. You may also (or instead) want to add as a focal point details to the design, perhaps in the railing or the flooring pattern, to break up the monotony and make the deck more interesting. A herringbone pattern in one section of the flooring would work, for instance, or a diamond or circle-shaped inset, or planters along the railing to frame the view. It is all about personal touches to make the deck more memorable.

TO BLEND OR TO CONTRAST? A deck that uses colors and materials that complement the house will make for a unified appearance. But you may prefer a deck that contrasts strongly with the house, to provide a sense of a different space and perhaps give the feel of a rustic retreat. In that case, natural wood is often the best choice. If the deck will not be on display to neighbors, a style disconnect need not feel awkward.

DECK HEIGHT. Most decks are near the height of the interior floor. You may want to step it down, however, for several reasons: a lower deck will be less likely to inhibit the view from inside. And if you go low enough—24 inches (61cm) or less above grade in most areas—you will not need a railing, which can make for a cleaner look and a simpler building process.

Decks built near ground level with no railing tend to visually emphasize the decking boards, while decks elevated a few feet (about 1m) have additional features that catch the eye, like the railing, stairs, and skirting. Decks higher than 6 feet (1.8m) aboveground usually have visible undersides. If your view of the deck from the backyard is private—that is, not visible from the street or sidewalk— you can permit yourself more creative latitude with the design, not worrying so much about its matching the house exterior.

LANDSCAPE. When first built, a deck may look a bit stark. But as nearby plants grow, the appearance can change dramatically. Tall plants near the fascia and shorter plants away from the fascia can gracefully draw the eye down to yard level. Similarly, wide stairs with room for planters can accomplish the same thing. Planters at railing or floor level help tie the deck into the landscape, especially if the colors of the plants or the design of the planters play off colors or structures in the yard.

THE VERTICAL STUFF. Decking is the dominant surface, of course, but railing, skirting, and fascia materials are actually more visible from outside the deck. The same is true of add-on features like planters, benches, or an overhead structure.

Check out the many railing possibilities available today. Older decks almost always had balusters (pickets) made of the same species of wood as the rails and the top cap, but these days metal balusters of various shapes and colors are popular. They not only perk up the visual appeal but also are usually more durable and sturdy.

Visual appeal. The elongated S-shape of this railing's balusters provides a dramatic design statement and welcome relief from the common square balusters seen on so many decks.

Consider the View

Many decks have a fundamental flaw—their railings, which are typically 42 inches (1.1m) high, block the view of the yard from inside the house and/or from a sitting position on the deck.

One solution is to make the railing nearly invisible. Railings made of tempered glass panels are literally see-through, but they require fastidious attention and cleaning. Horizontal cable rail systems or rails made of thin metal balusters (pickets) barely block the view.

Another approach is to lower the deck. If the deck is 3 feet (91cm) or more aboveground, lowering can have the added virtue of making the underside of the deck less visible. And if the lowered deck is less than 2 feet (61cm) aboveground, you will probably not need a railing at all; check with local codes.

To lower a deck, you may have two or three steps leading down from the house's door. Make the first step a landing that is at least 16 inches (40.6cm) wide to prevent tripping. Or build a series of level changes, perhaps cascading down to the lawn level. (As a

number of decks in this book show, creating different levels is also a good way to define different "rooms.")

In some cases, codes may allow you to install benches, which are typically 16 inches (40.6cm) tall, instead of railings to avoid blocking the view.

STYLE POINTS. If the style of your home is Victorian, Southwestern, Modern, or something else, how do you find a deck design that will blend? Often the way the deck is "framed" by its railing and trim elements will help establish a style connection with the house.

Contemporary homes have clean lines and simpler design elements. Metal cable or glass railing may be a good complement.

Traditional homes have more detail in the architecture or the decoration. For a Colonial home, consider white molded railings and decorative post caps. You can further beef up details by adding built-ins like benches or planters. For a Victorian home, look for molding, post caps, or balusters to echo the home's design.

DETAILS. The more you use your deck, the more you will appreciate any touches that add personality. Details bring a deck to another level. Sometimes you can add these after the basic deck is in place, as with planters, post or railing caps, or benches. Other times, you will make the call at the beginning of construction, as with the choice of fasteners, the distance between deck boards, or the choice of trim materials.

Take a look at other decks or at photos in this book to get an idea of which details will add the most bang for the buck. Hidden fasteners may be worth the extra expense, for instance, because they give the decking a cleaner look than exposed nails or screws. Next to the floor of the deck, the railing is probably the most visually noticeable section and a good place to spend extra for distinctive details. It is usually worth paying more for better-quality railing-top-cap lumber, for instance; this is also true for other noticeable places: the trim on top of a planter or built-ins for seating or storage.

Extreme style. The homeowners and deck designer-builder conspired to make a dramatic statement by incorporating in a radical way a favorite old tree into the deck's design.

Details make the difference. From the complementing brick and wood color to the choice of decking and the fine carpentry, the thought put into this deck is evident in the details.

Deck and Landscape

The contours of your yard can certainly affect your deck design. If your landscape is fairly level, construction should be uncomplicated. Slopes, even gradual ones, may require grading a level spot at the bottom or building a retaining wall. You may build a deck at the top of the slope, so its front will be raised high; depending on the situation, you may or may not need a set of stairs going down to the lawn. Or you can build a multilevel deck to take even better advantage of the site.

There is no rule that says a deck has to be attached to the house at all. You may find that a detached location, in the rear part of your yard, provides the perfect spot for a natural getaway.

Consider the features of your landscape—the slope of the grade, any existing vegetation, views, and climate. All of these can affect the design of your deck and where you build it. Do not draw the final plans until you have looked around your yard to see whether anything needs changing or not.

Work with nature, not against it. Trees, large stones, or other salient landscape features need not push your deck out of an otherwise perfect spot. With a little extra framing to support the decking, you can build your deck around the obstacle instead of trying to remove it. If you are building around a tree, check with a garden center to find out how much growth room the tree will need. Be careful to avoid damage to the tree during construction.

A slice of nature. The dark wood and rounded shapes used for this deck make it blend seamlessly with the natural beauty of the surrounding landscape.

Sun, Wind, and Rain

If the sun beats down on your deck mercilessly for most of the afternoon and early evening hours, you may not want to spend much time there. If you put the same deck where trees provide shelter from harsh sunlight, it will be much more enjoyable. Weather patterns can greatly affect the enjoyment of an outdoor space, and planning to minimize discomfort will ensure that your deck will be one that bustles with activity. Strategies range from simple umbrellas to substantial overheads. A well-placed pergola with open rafters or lattice roofing can provide dappled shade for a large deck. Lattice screens or fence panels tone down the wind (and add privacy). A small roofed structure over your dining spot lets you enjoy the space in inclement weather. A rollout awning can do the same job, and you can retract it when it is not needed.

Privacy plus. The slatted surround and overhead structure of this deck offer protection from the sun at certain times of the day and provide privacy as a bonus.

The Outdoor Rooms Approach

When space or budget is limited, some folks build a large rectangle and hope they can adjust use areas to fit afterward. But this is lazy planning and is likely to mean wasted or inadequate space and frustration. It is better to take the time to pencil in invisible walls and traffic paths you will need so that your deck will work well and make you happy; at the same time, consider modifying the overall design with bump-outs or angles to improve the sizing and flow of use areas. How much space do you need for various deck rooms? Some accumulated wisdom from deck builders follows.

DINING ROOM. A 12 x 12-foot (3.7m x 3.7m) area works for a round table for six; anything smaller will make it difficult to navigate around the table: for someone to reach or get out of a far seat, you may have to have other diners stand up and push in their chairs, or a server might have a hard time reaching the far end of the table. For best results, measure the area your table and chairs require and add 3 feet (91cm) on all sides so that you can slide chairs in and out. Some deck designs create a section with a bump-out, circular or angled, to accommodate the table and chairs.

COOKING. A space at least 5 x 10 feet (1.5m x 3m) will allow room for a cook plus a consultant or two. A small bump-out for a standalone grill is a popular feature of many deck designs. Or you may want to incorporate a full-blown outdoor kitchen (see page 19). Be sure your cooking area is not in a traffic path, and check that prevailing winds will not blow smoke toward diners or the back door of the house.

LOUNGING OR SUNNING. A comfortable reclining chair or two add welcome creature comforts to your deck. A small table nearby makes it the perfect spot to relax and read or soak in a few rays with your favorite beverage. A 5 x 8-foot (1.5m x 2.5m) area will handle one chair and a small table, and an 8 x 8-foot (2.5m x 2.5m) area is a good size for two chairs and a table.

Welcome. There is no mistaking this handsome deck for anything other than it is: a cozy outdoor "living room" complete with a welcoming stone fireplace.

Divided spaces. The deck's design and the furniture placement combine to create distinct social areas within this deck: conversational, lounging, dining, and cooking.

SPA OR HOT TUB. With a bit of adjacent seating, a spa or hot tub generally requires a 10-foot (3m) square area. Check whether you need additional space to store the cover when the spa is in use. And think about how to make it as easy as possible to get into and out of the spa.

TRAFFIC PATHS. Make sure people can move easily from one section, or "room," of the deck to another by allowing clear space for traffic paths. These should be 3 to 4 feet (91cm to 120cm) wide.

Outdoor Kitchens

Outdoor kitchens are growing in popularity, and people who have them rave about the convenience and entertainment possibilities. An outdoor kitchen gets the cook—and the mess—out of the home's main kitchen so that everyone can hang out together on the deck. Typical amenities include plenty of countertop space, grills and side burners, a refrigerator, a sink, and perhaps even a warming drawer, kegerator, or pizza oven.

Adding an outdoor kitchen may not be as expensive as you think, especially if you are willing to devote a couple of weekends to doing the work yourself. The biggest expense will be the grill, but the structure itself and other amenities like a sink, side burner, electric outlet, cabinets, pullout garbage, etc., are more affordable. And with planning, you can add amenities over time as funds become available.

Creative Homeowner's *Building Outdoor Kitchens for Every Budget* will help you choose inexpensive materials and perhaps build it yourself.

A kitchen counter on a deck is commonly built using wood or metal studs covered with concrete backer board and finished with stucco, tile, or faux stone. Countertops can be granite slab, tile, or concrete.

Be sure to position the counter and grill so that the grilling smoke will not bother diners or loungers. If a deck is small, you may choose to place them off the deck in a nearby spot, perhaps on a patio surface.

For food preparation, allow plenty of countertop space and at least 12 inches (30.5cm) on each side of the grill or burner. If you will use the kitchen at night, incorporate plenty of lighting.

Dining and Entertaining Options

The traditional dining table with chairs is what most people choose for everyday eating and dinner parties, but if you like buffet-style eating, you might prefer a living-room arrangement with comfortable chairs and side tables around a coffee table or fire pit. Larger decks often have multiple seating areas, sometimes built in or sometimes at a counter by the grill. Many people enjoy an open, spacious feel on their deck and want to minimize furnishings; for them, folding tables and chairs for special occasions are a good solution.

If parties are in your future, devise a clear strategy for entertaining. If you mainly expect smaller-size gatherings—maybe just a few people in addition to your family—a dining table that can accommodate a few extra chairs is a good choice. Many people position extra chairs along the side of the deck and pull them over to the table for company. For larger crowds, beefing up the seating with

additional portable tables and chairs is a popular solution. It usually works to create multiple small seating areas because people tend to break up into groups. And if you have extra-wide stairs, they will attract diners who enjoy a view that captures both yard and deck activity.

Many decks now have a space that is like a second living room, including sofas and overstuffed chairs. Increasingly, sound systems and weather-resistant televisions are appearing on decks. The old-fashioned drive-in movie experience has moved from the car to the deck, complete with s'mores cooked on the grill and blender beverages made in the outdoor kitchen. If this is how you would like to use your deck space and if space is limited, consider building a counter along the side of the deck for buffet-style eating and letting guests congregate in a deck living room to eat and relax.

Social graces. This stepped-down section of a large deck is perfectly designed for entertaining. There are seats for six, with plenty of horizontal space for resting drinks and finger food.

Ceilings and Walls

Many decks include an overhead structure, often called a pergola. If the sun will beat down on your deck, plan a pergola carefully so that it provides the right amount of shade when you want it. Of course, the closer together you place the top pieces, the more shade. But the position of the sun in the sky and the orientation of the boards will also affect how much dappled shade your deck will receive at different times of the day.

Trellis walls can provide for a windbreak and add privacy without seeming unfriendly. Avoid cheaply made, bargain priced trellis panels, which will look tacky in short order. Consider buying high-quality lattice panels. (Those that combine verticals with horizontals usually look classier than those with slats at 45-degree angles.) Or take the time to make custom lattice.

Rough and ready. Rustic and sturdy—and yes, beautiful—the roof over this deck comes complete with skylights to brighten the area while protecting it from the elements.

The Porch Option

More and more, people are choosing to have part of the deck covered by a roof and encased in screening. Once you do that, you have a "porch" rather than a "deck." A porch does not have the same open feel of a deck, but it has definite advantages. You can use it comfortably during a rainstorm or a buggy summer evening, and you can install an overhead fan/light and electrical receptacles for appliances.

One popular configuration is to place the porch section of the deck just outside the kitchen door, so you pass through it in order to get to the deck. That way, you have a gradual transition to the outdoors, and you do not have to get wet when you want to reach the deck on a rainy day.

Let there be light. Well-thought-out ambient and task lighting, as well as subtle accent lights, create an extraordinary mood on this deck while making it fully usable at night.

Lighting Options

Soft low-voltage lighting will make guests linger on your deck. You can install low-voltage or solar lights at various spots on the deck: railing posts (on the sides or tops), stair risers (recessed or surface-mounted), or pergola (overhead). In fact, local codes may require lights on step risers. You can also install landscaping lights in the ground near the deck or run your own cable after the deck is built by stapling low-voltage cable lights to the underside of the deck's railing or framing so it will be barely visible during the day while giving off plenty of light at night. If you plan this ahead of time, you can hide the cable in joists, posts, or other parts of the deck. If you have a means for stringing them, rope lights artfully dangled overhead add festive cheer.

You may want brighter task lights, which plug into a standard outlet, by the grill or food-prep counter; if you have an outdoor kitchen counter, you can add an outlet or two there, especially easy if the outdoor kitchen is located near the house.

Gardening

Plants and flowers make a deck feel more like a natural extension of the indoor living space and help tie everything together. Built-in planters and trellises are great for defining use areas on a deck by adding vertical walls. Tall foliage can provide relief from late afternoon sun, especially in the summer on south- or west-facing decks, while providing a sense of privacy. If the whole deck gets head-on afternoon sun, a pergola covered with vines may be a better solution.

A planter may hold soil directly, or it can be a cover for plastic pots. (That way, you can move plants around as they bloom.) Either way, provide drainage from both the planter and deck. Container plants require more water and fertilizer than in-ground plants. Check with your local gardening store for recommendations on soil mixtures and additives like water-absorbing polymer crystals, so your garden will grow better and be easier to maintain.

How It Is Put Together

The illustration below shows the basic elements of a typical deck. Not all decks have all of these parts, but your deck will have most of them. We will start at the bottom and work up.

A *pier*, also called a *footing*, is a solid piece of concrete that supports the *structural posts*. The size and shape of the footings, as well as whether they rise aboveground or not and whether the posts rest on or in them, are determined by local codes. If footings rise aboveground and the posts rest on top, you must install metal post anchors, which keep the posts from moving and hold the bottoms of the posts slightly above the concrete so they can dry out.

Structural posts, which support the deck, are typically made of 4x4 (10cmx10cm) or 6x6 (15cmx15cm) pressure-treated lumber. A *girder*, also called a *beam*, is usually made of two or three 2-bys (5cm-bys) laminated together. The girder supports the *joists*, regularly spaced 2-by (5cm-by) boards that support the decking. (Most builders place girders under the deck framing, but some builders install a *flush beam* at the same level as the joists, which are attached to the beam via joist hangers.) Sometimes short pieces of *bridging*, or *blocking*, made of the same material as the joists, are attached as shown along the middle of the joist run to provide extra strength and stability.

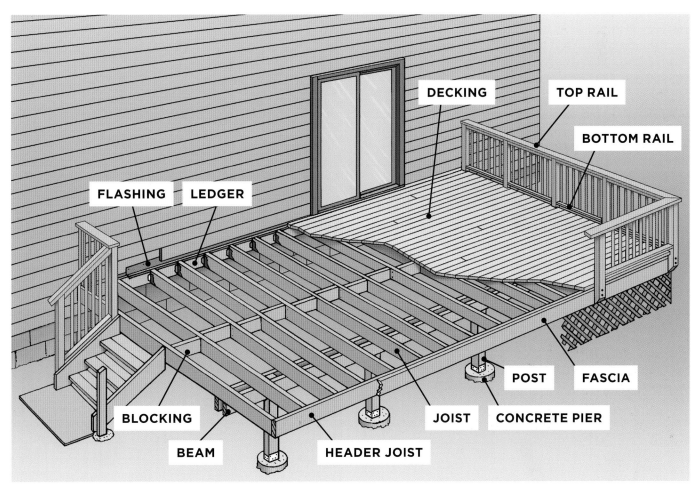

Anatomy of a deck. Every deck needs "bones," and here the major structural members of the typical deck are called out.

At the house, the joists usually tie to a *ledger* board, which attaches to the house. If the house's siding is cut out to accommodate the ledger, metal or plastic *flashing* is used to waterproof the joint. In the case of a freestanding deck, there is a girder (with footings and posts) near the house and no ledger. *Outside joists* and the *header joist* form the outside frame of the structure. *Fascia* boards usually dress up the outside and header joists. *Decking boards* sit on top of the joists and are fastened with screws, nails, or special hidden fasteners. Wood decking is typically made of 5/4x6 (3cmx15cm) or 2x6 (5cmx15cm) lumber. Hardwood decking is often 1-by (2.5cm-by) boards, which are actually ¾ inch (2cm) thick. Composite decking is typically 1 inch (2.5cm) thick and 6 inches (15cm) wide.

A common railing arrangement, shown here, employs 4x4 (10cmx10cm) *rail posts*, which attach to a horizontal *top and bottom rail*. Wood or metal *balusters*, also called pickets, are evenly spaced between the railing posts. A rail cap tops the whole thing off.

Stairs are constructed with downward-angled 2x12s (5cmx30cm) called *stringers*, which support *treads* (which you step on). The width of the stairs determines the number of stringers necessary. A tread is commonly made of a single 2x12 (5cmx30cm) or a pair of 2x6s (5cmx15cm). *Risers*, usually made of 1x8 (2.5cmx20cm), often cover the vertical spaces between the treads.

Holding up the deck. Structural posts, along with the beams, or girders, form the key supporting framework of a deck, especially an elevated one. Here the posts are braced until the concrete foundations firm up.

House support. The ledger is bolted to the headers or rim joists of the house for firm support. The decks joists join the ledgers via metal brackets that attach to the ledger.

Metal's mettle. In this unusual configuration, the deck's support system is a prefabricated metal system. The deck's joists rest on top of the metal girder.

All beamed up. A massive 4-by (10cm-by) wood beam shoulders the weight of the elevated deck, supported by 4-by (10cm-by) wood posts.

Joist hardware. Sometimes, especially in seismically active areas, joists need extra stabilization. Though fully supported by beams, these joists also have special metal ties to hold them in place.

Hanger hardware. Joist hangers come in sizes to accommodate all dimensions of structural lumber, most commonly 2x8 (5cmx20cm), 2x10 (5cmx25cm), and 2x12 (5cmx30cm).

Notched support. Some builders notch support posts, especially in the middle of a beam's span, but full post support with saddle hardware is usually the best way to go.

Extra framing support. Angled decking needs additional joists where the decking meets in a V-shape to provide extra nailing surface.

Budget Often Determines Deck Size and Materials

Calculating a construction budget entails three variables:

1. Cost

2. Square footage

3. Quality of materials

Any two of these variables will produce the third, but you can't control all three simultaneously. Many people start out with a target price, so they may have to compromise on either size or materials. If, for instance, you know for certain the size deck you need and the amount of money you can spend, you will have to choose materials that fall within the budget.

If you experience sticker shock, you have discovered a design limitation. You may want to go smaller. A bigger deck isn't always the best solution, even with an unlimited budget. An intelligent, aesthetically pleasing design may give you more bang for the buck.

Another general rule of thumb: if you hire a builder, the total deck cost will usually be about three times the cost of materials. (Builders often use this formula: one third for materials; one-third for labor; and one-third for the building company—that is, for profit and the cost of doing business.) You may be able to get a larger or better deck by doing at least some of the work yourself.

RIGHT-SIZE BOARDS. Beams and joists must be wide enough (and in the case of beams, thick enough) to support the deck's load. The required width of framing members—whether they are 2x6s (5cmx15cm), 2x8s (2cmx20cm), and so on—depends on the distance they must travel, or their *span*. Your local building department will have a span chart, which describes what size boards you need to use for your design. A good builder may exceed recommendations and install joists and beams that are more substantial than required.

LEDGER. Most decks attach to the house via a ledger, which is a crucial structural element. A ledger must be strong and water resistant. Opinions differ on how to install ledgers, but you should check you local codes because they may specify the method you will need to use for your deck.

Meeting Code

Whether you are building yourself or hiring a pro, be sure that your deck meets local building codes. You will need to satisfy a building inspector, who will most likely zero in on the footings and posts, ledger and flashing, joist sizing and spacing, stairway, and railing. Get your plans approved by the building department ahead of time, and post a permit. You will probably need to schedule and pass two or more inspections.

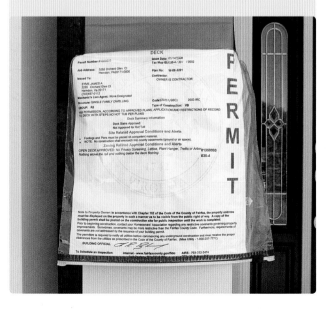

If you have wood or vinyl siding, some contractors prefer to cut the siding out and attach the ledger to the house's sheathing. The cutout makes the house vulnerable to water damage, so it is critical to install substantial metal or plastic flashing to keep water out. Some builders do not cut out the siding; instead, they snug the ledger to the house. Others use a "hold-off" method, which separates the ledger from the siding so that the area can dry out between rains.

Most builders install ledgers using heavy-duty lag screws driven into the house's framing. Special ¼-inch (0.5cm) "ledger lock" screws seem to work best, but some codes demand ⅓-inch (0.8cm) lag screws. In some areas, strict codes demand that bolts run through the house's framing and into the basement or crawl space, fastened by locknuts.

FOOTINGS AND POSTS. Here is another area where opinions vary. Some people are dead set against exposing any lumber to ground contact because the moisture it encounters can cause rot. They advocate that footings should rise aboveground and posts should rest on top of the footings so that the wood can dry out. Another approach is to pour concrete footings, the tops of which are 1 foot (30.5cm) or more underground, set posts on top of the footings, and tamp soil around the bottom of the posts. Those who advocate for in-ground posts say that the method has two advantages: it anchors the deck against wind shear and enables posts to resist rot for a long time. In the end, you may not have a choice; local building codes may require you to install footings and posts in a certain way.

PROTECTING YOUR DECK. A poorly constructed deck can start to rot—or can cause rot to appear on the house—within a few years. Cracks may also appear. Be sure to take steps to keep your boards in sound condition.

The builders in this book take the steps necessary to ensure that decking, railings, and structural members all stay strong and good-looking for decades. They come from various parts of the country and choose materials and techniques that are the most durable in their climates. In some areas water is the main enemy, while in other places harsh sun causes the most damage. Either way, it is important to install boards that are made for outdoor use and to seal (and perhaps also stain) them regularly if needed.

Structural and Visible Materials

Pressure-treated lumber is the near-universal choice for deck structures. But not all treated lumber is created equal. Some types will be durable—rot-free, straight, and free of cracks and other problems—while lesser boards may cause problems down the road when they warp or crack.

WOOD SPECIES. In much of the country, southern yellow pine (SYP) is the standard wood species for treated lumber. It is strong and stable, and it accepts the treatment readily. In some regions (especially in the West) southern yellow pine is not available, and Douglas fir or "hem-fir" lumber is used instead. Douglas fir is very strong and stable but doesn't accept the treatment easily, so it usually contains a pattern of incisions made during the treating process to aid in absorption of the treatment solution. These incisions will not disappear over time.

"Hem-fir" is a general designation that can refer to several possible species. Some of these are reliable sources, while others are prone to problems, especially warping. Before buying hem-fir, consult with local dealers, builders, or your inspector to be sure it will be strong and straight.

WOOD GRADING. Copper, the main ingredient in most treated lumber, is expensive, so manufacturers inject only as much as they need to. Most treated lumber is rated for "aboveground" use only, meaning it should not touch soil and should not be put where water will puddle for extended periods of time. For boards that will go into the ground (or even come close to the ground) or be exposed to persistent moisture, use lumber rated for "ground contact."

A board's grading is also important. Boards rated *No. 2* or better will usually perform well. Lower grades may warp, crack, or decay. *Select* or *No. 1* lumber is even better. The best boards are rated *KDAT* (kiln-dried after treatment) or *S-Dry*; they are low in moisture content, so they are unlikely to warp or shrink.

Preservative Types and Safety

Older treated lumber used chromated copper arsenate (CCA) preservative, which contains arsenic and chromium. In 2003, it was essentially banned for residential use. If you have old CCA lumber, it is not a danger under normal circumstances because the preservative bonds firmly to wood fibers. If you cut the lumber, however, the sawdust can cause rashes in some adults and can be a health risk for small children.

Newer treatments are copper based, which can make them expensive because the price of copper sometimes soars. The treatments use *micronized copper* and may go by the designation MCQ or MCA. The U.S. Environmental Protection Agency (EPA) has registered the treatments, declaring them as generally considered safe. There may be hazards when the wood is burned, however, or if contact is made with the sawdust. To be safe, food or soil used to grow food should not come into contact with treated lumber.

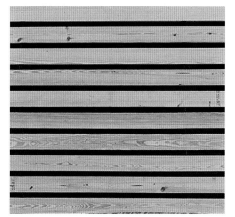

Number 1 grade of most common lumber has few, if any, knots.

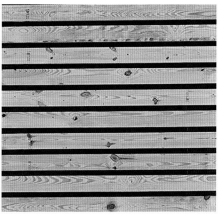

Number 2 grade has more knots and defects than Number 1. It's the type specified as a minimum requirement in most building codes.

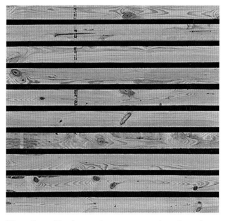

Number 3 of most common lumber has many knots and defects. It may not be approved by your local building code.

When it comes to the lumber used for decking, railings, fascia, and skirting—all the material you will see—there are quite a few options. Take into account the cost of future maintenance as well as the initial cost of the materials. Synthetic lumber is expensive, but you can keep it looking new with a sweep and an occasional wash. Cedar and treated lumber are less expensive but need to be stained and sealed regularly. Ironwoods are roughly the same cost as synthetics but also need to be sealed every year or so. You can seal the wood yourself or spend the extra few hundred dollars to hire a contractor to do it.

SYNTHETIC DECKING. Composite and vinyl decking and railing components are extremely popular in many parts of the country. Composite lumber combines plastic (often but not always recycled) with wood fibers. Vinyl lumber is made of "virgin" (non-recycled) plastic.

Quite a few synthetic-lumber companies are vying for your business, and their products differ. Many types have a faux wood-grain texture, while others are smoother. Some have a single color, but boards with variegated colors that mimic the look of natural wood are increasingly popular. You may choose to use one type of composite on the deck and another for the railing or fascia.

Many early types of synthetics had serious problems, but most products available today are higher in quality and have proved themselves over time. Still, some types may fade in color, swell when wet, easily scratch or stain, and attract mildew and mold. So choose carefully: select a product with a proven track record in your area. A high-quality product may offer a 25-year warranty.

IRONWOODS. Also called Brazilian or tropical hardwood, species that go by names like ipé, cumaru, and pau lopé are extremely strong and virtually free of knots; they will remain rot-free for many decades. Ironwood is usually similar in price to synthetics but may cost more to install because it is so hard, requiring the extra labor of predrilling for every nail or other fastener. It is possible to let ironwood weather to a silvery gray, but most people choose to maintain its dark good looks by staining and/or sealing it yearly.

Ipé and other ironwoods are usually sold in boards ¾ inch (2cm) thick and 5½ inches (14cm) wide (1x6, or 2.5cmx15cm). Because it is so strong, it need not be thicker for decking. Other sizes, such as 2-bys (5cm-bys) and 4x4s (10cmx10cm), are also available for railings and trim.

CEDAR. Western red cedar is a fairly inexpensive option. It is often available as 5/4 *decking*, which is 1 inch (2.5cm) thick and 5½ inches (14cm) wide (5/4x6, or 3cmx15cm), with rounded edges. You can also buy cedar 2-bys (5cm-bys) and 4x4s (10cmx10cm). Most cedar contains knots and color variations. If you seal it regularly and install it where it can dry out after rains, cedar can last a long time. There are various grades; "tight-knot" cedar is recommended.

REDWOOD. Once a very common decking option, redwood now has limited availability and may be quite expensive in some locales. Choose a grade that is all or mostly composed of the dark "heart" of the wood; the light-colored sapwood will rot quickly. You can re-stain redwood yearly or allow it to go gray.

TREATED DECKING. Pressure-treated decking and fascia boards are not nearly as popular as they once were, but remain a good option for a low-cost deck. If you use good-quality treated southern yellow pine (preferably KDAT), you can apply special stains made for use with treated lumber (typically with a bit more red tint) to produce attractive decking.

Star bright. In another view of the deck from page 12, the inlaid star fully displays its fanciful touch. The synthetic decking is beautiful and practical because it will keep its good looks for many years to come—with little maintenance.

Stairway to... This spiral staircase leads from the slate-covered patio to the upper deck. The underside of the deck is even finished—with varnished cedar.

The height of elegance. The color combinations of the reddish synthetic decking, terra-cotta tones in the stonework, copper torchieres, and beige stucco spell sophistication.

Relaxing retreat. This counter with a stone facade and granite countertop is a good solution for a deck's "outdoor kitchen" and entertainment area.

PART TWO:
Meet the Builders

For this, the all-new fourth edition of the Creative Homeowner *Deck Designs* book, we chose five of the country's best deck builders from various regions. Joel Boyer works in the Chicago area; Ivan Arana hails from the Maryland/Washington, D. C., region; Barry Streett designs in the Denver area; Gustavo "Gus" de la Cruz is from central New Jersey; and Deanne and Scott Clough represent the Marin County area in California. Their designs represent styles popular in their locales but would work well in any part of the country. Many of the decks are newly built, and many have been around two years or more.

For each of the five builders, you will first find a section discussing his design approaches and a gallery showing off his work. You will also learn about his signature building techniques—which often go above and beyond code requirements to achieve really great decks.

Then you will find, for each of the builders, detailed treatments of specific decks. Photos show the overall plan of the deck, as well as details and special features. Drawings and a section on building show generally how the deck is put together. Each of the designer-builders has a website with more details about his company. And each is happy to hear from you via email or a phone call should you want to purchase a complete plan or—if you live in their area—hire him to build a deck.

Joel Boyer builds in the Chicago area.

Ivan Arana builds in the Maryland/Washington D. C. area.

Gustavo "Gus" de la Cruz creates decks in central New Jersey.

Barry Streett works in and around Denver.

Scott and Deanne Clough build in and around Marin County, California.

Unique Deck Builders

In 1982, Joel Boyer started what he thought would be a short-lived business building decks. At that time in the Chicago area, a deck was thought of as a simple tack-on, perhaps a place to keep the garbage and maybe support a picnic table and a cart grill. But over time, Midwesterners gained a greater appreciation for the delights of outdoor living—after all, even in cold Chicago a deck can be enjoyed seven or more months a year. So Boyer, along with his growing clientele, learned that a deck can be a thing of beauty and a platform for gracious entertainment and relaxation. And his business blossomed into a career dedicated to making people happy.

His customers are usually young to middle-aged professionals. Most want a deck that is an extension of their home, providing extra living space for family gatherings and occasional parties.

Because he builds high-quality, durable decks, much of his business comes from word of mouth. He has become a second- and even third-generation builder—some of his current clients are children or even grandchildren of his earlier clients.

He has a pretty large operation, typically keeping three or more crews busy. Each crew has at least one highly experienced carpenter, usually with twenty-five or more years of experience. Decks are his mainstay, but during the winter he also does remodeling work. Unusual among deck builders, he has a 2,000-square-foot (185.8m^2) showroom that displays ipé, cedar, and composite decking materials, as well as a variety of railing styles and overhead possibilities.

As of this writing, Boyer generally charges about $18 per square foot (0.09m^2) for a pressure-treated deck; $22 for a cedar deck, and $37 for an ipé or composite deck. Vertical components like lattice and railings, as well as amenities like built-in benches, will influence the price.

Angled decking. A jagged series of angles nicely frames the pool and helps define several use areas.

Joel Boyer

UNIQUE DECK BUILDERS

Highland Park, IL
847-831-1388 | 800-427-DECK | 800-TREX-PRO
www.uniquedeck.com

THE OVERALL DESIGN

Boyer finds that customers today want deck designs with an organic, free-flowing feel. A deck needs to effortlessly extend the indoor living space and provide a natural-feeling entry to the yard. That means there should be ample space for outdoor furniture and cooking areas. It also means that landscaping is integral to the overall plan.

He always makes an at-home visit with a prospective customer, where he works to gain an idea of the family's needs and wants. He talks the customer through the design process, learning things such as how large an area they need, how much of the deck should be in the sun, and how much should be shaded. He starts with a pencil or simple computer drawing of the deck. Once things are basically hammered out, he is usually able to produce a detailed drawing within five days.

He makes sure that traffic can flow easily into and out of the house and allows for passing areas between dining and lounging portions of the deck that are at least 3 feet (91cm) wide. Stairways are almost always 4 feet (120cm) wide so that people can pass each other going in opposite directions.

Color and texture are as important as shape and size. He works to give the customer a clear idea how the decking and railing will look after they have been stained and finished. He comes to the house equipped with an iPad that is loaded with images of various wood and stain possibilities to help them choose on site. Customers who are still unsure of finish material choices can visit his showroom to get a better idea how their deck will look.

ALL THE ANGLES. Though there is nothing wrong with running decking parallel or perpendicular to the house, he almost always runs decking at various angles. In many cases, a change of angle signifies a different area of the deck—for instance, one angle for a lounging area, and another angle for the cooking or dining areas.

KITCHENS AND OTHER AMENITIES. Boyer also installs outdoor kitchens (some of which can be seen in Creative Homeowner's *Building Outdoor Kitchens for Every Budget*). Because he typically designs and builds the kitchen at the same time as the deck, the kitchen counter and grill are positioned for ease of use and unimpeded traffic flow.

His kitchen counters almost always feature a high-quality grill and at least 5 feet (1.5m) of counter space. The kitchens are usually fairly modest in size, features, and price—as opposed to the $50,000-and-up kitchens that people build in other parts of the country. Other amenities include access doors and drawers, refrigerators, TVs and stereo systems, and electrical receptacles for appliances. He sometimes installs a sink and refrigerator, but most of his customers do not consider these necessary.

He often incorporates built-in benches, decks, and planters, but doesn't overdo it: a few built-ins lend the feel of a living room, but too many would be constraining; people prefer to accessorize with furniture and personal touches of their choosing.

Custom woodworking. Careful woodworking makes all of these angled ironwood boards line up perfectly.

Cascading stairs. In this small space, a set of cascading stairs makes a stunning design statement and provides a fun spot for people to sprawl out while socializing.

Trellis and overhead. In this city space, a combination of overhead and lattice wall provides just the right amount of privacy, while still preserving a nice open view. This lattice is pretty enough to enjoy on its own but would also look great with vine growth.

Parquet rooftop. Parquet flooring and a latticework fence bring the warmth of wood tones to this rooftop deck to create a comfortable and attractive room with a view.

TRELLISES. Many of Joel's decks include vertical trellis walls. He avoids using standard 45-degree crisscross trellis panels, which are inexpensive—and look that way. Instead he often installs panels made of clear cedar in a rich pattern of variously spaced pieces that run vertically and horizontally; or, he custom makes trellises. This is definitely worth the extra expense, because the quality in the details elevates the overall appearance of the deck, especially for vertical elements at eye level.

Trellis sections are not for every deck, but they can help define space, add privacy without seeming unfriendly, and provide dappled partial shade—welcome on hot days.

CITY DECKS. Boyer works both in the northern suburbs of Chicago, where houses often have spacious yards, and within city limits, where space is at a premium. Sometimes this means working carefully to design a deck for a small backyard that maximizes usable space.

Another option is a rooftop deck. In Chicago (and other cities as well), it is fairly common to have a garage with a flat roof, which can be used for a deck. Rooftop decks give urbanites breathing space and open up a whole new view of their neighborhoods.

FINISH MATERIALS

Though there is a growing demand for composite and vinyl decking and railings, natural wood is still the more popular choice in Chicago. For many years Joel built most of his decks of western red cedar, and it is still popular. Lately, however, many customers have opted for Brazilian hardwoods such as ipé or pau lopé.

Cedar has got something of a bum rap lately. It is somewhat soft and will develop rot if not adequately sealed. However, people who do not inflict more than usual wear and tear on a deck find that it stays dent-free for a long time. (If, however, you have large dogs or your children will play roughly on the deck, you may want to go with a harder material.) If you keep cedar protected with stain and sealer, it will stay rot-free for decades. A possible exception is boards that come into contact with the ground or boards installed where water will collect and puddle: those boards may need to be replaced after 10 years or so. Boyer uses high-quality cedar that is rated "select tight-knot."

Many of his customers prefer ironwood or composites; see pages 28–29 for more information on them.

For railings, Boyer usually uses balusters (pickets) made of aluminum or other rustproof materials. Metal balusters are more expensive than wood but are much more durable: they won't rot or come loose over the years.

Boyer's Techniques

1 Because the Chicagoland area experiences temperatures ranging from below zero to one hundred plus, together with highly variable humidity levels, decks must be built with stable, strong materials. Boyer always uses expensive, high-quality No. 1 southern yellow pine treated framing lumber that is kiln-dried after treatment (KDAT). The lumber is resistant to warping, shrinking, and cracking, even in extreme weather.

2 He avoids hiring subcontractors as much as possible. The reason: quality control. Boyer likes to take total responsibility for the job. By using his own trained crew, he knows that they will arrive on time, and he won't need to blame someone else if something goes wrong.

3 Boyer is dedicated to finishing in a timely manner. He makes sure a crew completes a deck before moving on to the next job.

4 In compliance with local codes, most of his post footings are 42 inches (1.1m) deep. Where in other parts of the country in-ground posts are common, he is usually required by codes to pour a footing that rises above the ground and rest the post on a post anchor that is on top of the footing.

5 Most of his decks are built against homes that are masonry, so he usually attaches the ledger using lag screws driven into lag shields in the concrete or brick. Even where there is wood or vinyl siding, he avoids cutting out the siding to avoid damaging the house's underlying sheathing.

6 For the area under the deck, he applies commercial-grade weed fabric, covered with at least 2 inches (5cm) of #7 stone to prevent weed growth.

7 For a finished appearance, Boyer usually installs solid skirting running from the bottom of the decking to a couple of inches (about 5cm) above the ground. The skirting is usually 1x8 (2.5cmx20cm), with only ⅛-inch (0.3cm) spaces between the boards. In the Midwest this provides all of the breathing space needed. If you live in a humid or rainy area, you may need more space for better air circulation.

8 When building on a roof, Boyer has developed building methods that are durable and leave the roof waterproof. He also builds in "pods" so that sections can be removed for future deck repairs if they are needed.

Split-Level with Wood Bar and Spa

From a 10 x 22-foot (3m x 6.7m) upper deck with just enough space for a bar table and kitchen island, two sets of stairs lead down to a larger 16 x 34-foot (4.9m x 10.4m) deck that has plenty of space for a dining room and a spa with seating—and even some extra room for lounge chairs. Classic joinery and a few angles make the design more interesting and lend a craftsman-like feel.

The Design

This largish deck provides at least five use areas: a barbecue island, a bar table, a dining area, a space for lounge chairs, and a spa with nearby seating.

VIEW AND TRAFFIC FLOW. The deck is orientated toward a lake view, and most of the seating enables people to gaze at the water, the expanse of lawn, and the boathouse. Those sitting at the bar have perhaps the best view, but diners and loungers below can also enjoy it.

Stairs on each side of the upper deck lead to the backyard, and stairs on the front of the upper deck lead to the lower deck. This allows for easy traffic flow, even when the deck is fully occupied.

The decking is ipé, attached with barely visible decking screws. It has been lightly stained and sealed with a product that barely changes its natural color.

UPPER DECK. The smaller upper deck is wide enough to allow people to carry food to and from the barbecue. Its decking runs at an angle in one direction, while the decking below runs in the opposite direction.

The barbecue counter is 6 feet (1.8m) long and a little more than 2 feet (61cm) wide, with a large-capacity gas grill in the middle. A granite countertop on each side gives the cook handy places to rest meat and vegetables before and after cooking, as well as a drink or snack to enjoy while cooking. (If you also want space for preparing a salad or veggies, you will probably want a longer counter.) The door below the grill could have been stainless steel, but cedar is much less expensive and adds a nice warm touch.

The bar table is 42 inches (1.1m) tall and about 18 inches (45.7cm) wide—just right for a drink and perhaps a small plate of hors d'oeuvres or tapas. It is made of the same ipé as the decking, and should be sealed with a food-safe product, such as mineral oil or bar wax. If your stools or chairs are shorter, adjust the height of the table accordingly.

Strong decking. Ironwood is hard and strong enough that you need not worry about scratches from pet claws.

SPA AND LOUNGE AREA. The spa is placed on a peninsula that is essentially a half octagon but with sides of uneven length. A nearby bench, facing toward the house, is often used for draping towels but also offers a nice place for non-soakers to converse with soakers. A set of two steps makes it easy to enter the spa.

To the side of the spa is a space about 12 feet (3.7m) long where a set of lounge chairs with a coffee table fit nicely, without hindering traffic flow. Spaces like this may appear "blank" on your deck's plan drawings, but it is important to make them large enough for furniture.

Spa and lounge area. This spa area makes it easy for folks to jump into and out of the water and provides several places for non-soakers to sprawl out.

Strategic built-ins. This bench does not get used as a seat very often, but it has two practical uses: it is near the barbecue, so platters of food can be set there; and it partially hides the gas meter while still allowing it be read.

Skirting. A combination of solid and latticework skirting reaches all the way to the ground, giving the deck a neat, finished appearance.

DINING AREA. There is enough deck width for a dining table and chairs, with room for passing traffic on the house side of the table but not on the other side, where it is not needed. The deck is cut off at a 45-degree angle, which adds flair to the design and helps define space for a round table. If you want a rectangular table, you would probably be better off not eliminating the corner.

RAILING AND SKIRTING. The railing is made of more ipé. The top cap is 5½-inch-wide (14cm) decking, which is wide enough for setting a drink but not for most potted plants or food platters. The balusters are black powder-coated aluminum; a touch of black always looks classy next to natural wood.

At the stairways, Joel capped the railing posts with simple newels made of decking pieces with corners cut off at 45 degrees. Where the top cap runs over railing posts, the cap pieces are joined with carefully cut miter joints for a neat look. The miter joints are held together with several screws facing in different directions so they cannot come apart.

The deck features solid skirting on the sides, made of closely spaced vertical 1x6s (2.5cmx15cm), and latticework on the front. Both lattice and solid skirting are made of cedar, which is slightly lighter in color than the decking.

Building the Deck

This is a two-level deck, with the bottom level three wide steps down.
A spa, installed on top of the decking, will likely require extra support.

FRAMING. Here (and for all of Boyer's decks) the posts rest on raised footings, so treated lumber rated for "aboveground" is suitable everywhere. If your posts come into contact with the soil, be sure to use lumber rated for ground contact.

Attach and flash the ledger, following local codes to securely anchor it and keep the house dry. The upper deck is about 1½ inches (4cm) below the door's threshold to keep snow and rain from entering the house easily. Install the ledger lower than that by one deck board's thickness. Measure and dig holes for two rows of footings, for the two beams. It may be easiest to pour the concrete for these footings now, or you can do it after framing. There are eight more footings needed to support the framing around the perimeter; you may dig them now or after you have built the framing because you will easily be able to get access to the area. Codes may require you to add additional footings, posts, and perhaps a beam to support the spa. The beam closest to the house supports both levels.

Build the joist framing on temporary supports, and then add the posts and beams later. Build the frame for the upper level, attaching the joists to the ledger via joist hangers at the house and installing a header joist at the other end. Build the lower frame with its header joist directly below so that both can be supported with one beam.

A standard step is 7½ inches (19.1cm) tall, so build the lower level three steps, or 22½ inches (54.6cm), below the upper level. Construct the framing on temporary supports, with doubled outside joists. Dig holes for posts that will support the doubled outside joists at the corners.

SUPPORTING THE SPA. A spa filled with water and people can weigh 5,000 pounds or so. If the spa will rest on top of the deck, the underlying framing must be exceptionally strong. Here, a beam runs under the middle of the spa. Depending on soil conditions and local codes, you may need to add another beam with posts and footings. You may also need to make the postholes under the spa larger than the other postholes, and fill them with double the amount of concrete. In this case, doubling the joists under the spa was enough support to satisfy the building inspector.

DECKING, RAILING, AND FASCIA. Decking runs at a 45-degree angle. Cut a number of decking boards at 45 degrees on one end, where they will meet the house siding. For each section, first install a long board near the middle. Check it for straightness using a string line, and measure to be sure it is at 45 degrees to the house. Then use decking spacers to install the other pieces, with ⅛-inch (0.3cm) gaps between the boards. Wherever possible, allow boards to "run wild" past the end of the deck; mark a row of them with a chalk line, and cut them all at once.

Notch the decking where the railing posts will go. Notch the posts, and install them using lag screws driven into the doubled outside joists. Also install 4x4 (10cmx10cm) posts for the eating bar. First attach wood cleats as needed so that the posts will be firmly anchored.

To build the railing, cut 2x4 (5cmx10cm) top and bottom rails to fit between posts (keeping in mind the thickness of the railing brackets). Lay them out on the deck, and attach the balusters between them, spaced evenly, using the hardware that slips onto the balusters. Set each baluster section in place, and attach it using the railing brackets. Install railing cap made of decking carefully cut to form tight joints. Drill pilot holes, and drive screws in two or more directions to fasten the top cap securely. Cut and install pieces of decking to cap off the tops of the posts at the stairways.

STAIRS. At the bottom of the two narrow sets of stairs on each side, dig postholes and install 4x4 (10cmx10cm) posts in concrete. Make stringers, and attach them to the framing at the top and to the posts sunk in concrete at the bottom. (If you want to use a poured concrete slab at the bottom of the stairs, you can rest the stringers on that instead.) Install treads made of two decking pieces each and risers made of cedar 1x8 (2.5cmx20cm).

For the two steps that lead to the lower level, make box framing similar to that shown on page 82. Install decking for the treads. Attach cleats as needed, and install vertical pieces of cedar 1x8 (2.5cmx20cm) to cover the space between the two levels.

Run horizontal 2x4s (5cmx10cm) or other framing between the posts at the bottom, to which you can attach the bottoms of the skirting boards. Depending on the situation, you may install the skirting boards (or lattice panels, in front) first and then the fascia, or vice versa.

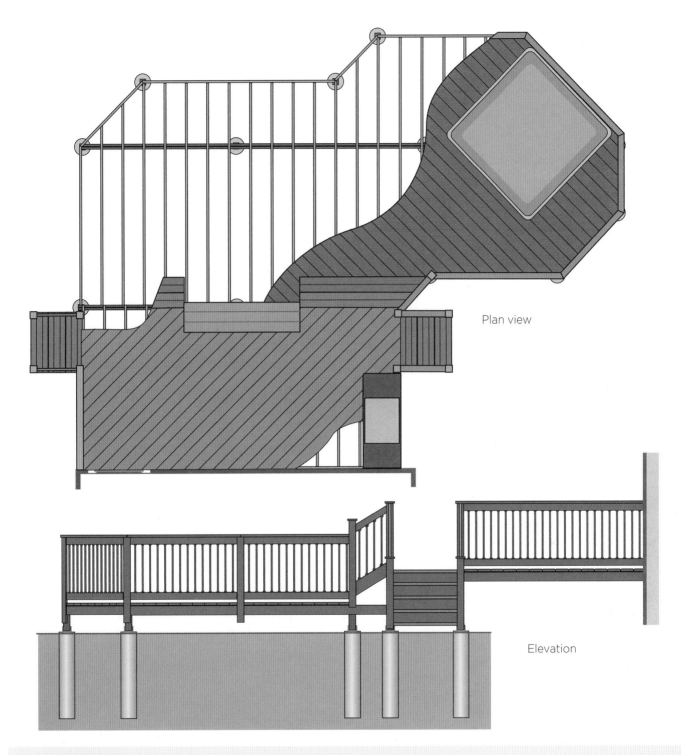

Plan view

Elevation

MATERIALS

» FRAMING (ALL TREATED)
- ❑ 4x4 (10cmx10cm) posts
- ❑ 2x8s (5cmx20cm) for ledger and joists
- ❑ Double 2x8s (5cmx20cm) for beams
- ❑ 2x12 (5cmx30cm) stair stringers
- ❑ Joist hangers

» FOOTINGS
- ❑ Concrete
- ❑ Tube forms
- ❑ Metal post anchors

» DECKING AND FASCIA
- ❑ 1x6 (2.5cmx15cm) ipé decking

» RAILING
- ❑ 4x4 (10cmx10cm) ipé posts
- ❑ 2x4 (5cmx10cm) ipé for top and bottom rails
- ❑ 1x6 (2.5cmx15cm) ipé decking for cap rail
- ❑ Powder-coated metal balusters

Cozy Retreat

A deck does not have to be large or full of fancy angles to give you what you want. This modestly sized (and priced) deck extends a kitchen bump-out in the house design and looks like a natural addition to the house exterior. It has room for barbecuing, dining for six, and a bit of potting.

Grill area. A grill with wing shelves fits snugly. A built-in counter could be placed here later to increase countertop and storage space.

The Design

This deck is simplicity itself: a basic rectangle divided into two neatly apportioned sections. Directly off the kitchen door is an upper section, about 6 x 10 feet (1.8m x 3m), with room for a grill with wings. The lower section, just one step down, is 10 x 20 feet (3m x 6m), the right size for a rectangular dining table. A set of stairs, just to the left of the upper area, leads down to a paver patio.

Even a small deck, if planned carefully, can make it easy for people to move around. Because of the stairs' location, traffic flows easily from the kitchen door to the grill, to the table, or down the stairs. The cook, and perhaps a helper, will not interfere with people going to other areas. The 10-foot (3m) width of the dining area leaves enough room for a server to move around seated diners on one side but not the other.

The upper deck is dropped one step down, or 7½ inches (19.1cm), from the house, and the lower deck is another step down. The resulting 15-inch (38.1cm) drop improves the view of the yard from inside the house; otherwise, the railing would be in the way.

FINISH MATERIALS. All of the finish wood is light-colored cedar, which makes a small deck feel larger than darker decking would. The tight knots of these boards (graded Select) are reminiscent of old-fashioned cabin paneling. Because the knots are tight, you need not fear they will fall out—as might happen with lesser grade cedar. A light semi-transparent stain/sealer should be reapplied least once a year.

The railing wraps around the grill, where it provides a welcome bit of shelf space. The balusters are black aluminum in a square shape, so they contrast in color, but complement the overall shape of the deck.

THE PERGOLA. Overhead is a pergola that provides dappled shade and a sense of enclosure. Its 4x4 (10cmx10cm) posts also act as railing posts. Double 2x8s (5cmx20cm), attached to each side of the posts with curve-cut ends, serve as beams. On top of the beams are 2x8 (5cmx20cm) rafters, then 2x2 (5cmx5cm) top pieces, all spaced 16 inches (40.6cm) apart. The square lattice skirting at the bottom includes two access doors opening to handy storage space.

The pergola. Beam ends cut in an ogee shape add welcome curves to the overall design and give a sense of flight to the pergola.

Dining area. No space is wasted in the dining area, which has just the right amount of room for the rectangular table.

Lattice and rail. Square lattice skirting reaches nearly to the ground. Railing posts are notched at the bottom so they feel more like part of the deck.

Building the Deck

Use kiln-dried No. 1 or No. 2 pressure-treated lumber for the framing. Also choose high-quality, tight-knot cedar decking, as well as rough-side cedar for the fascia.

FRAMING. On the upper section, attach the ledger with flashing 2½ inches (6.5cm) below the house's threshold so that the finished deck surface will be about 1½ inches (4cm) below the threshold. Install the lower ledger 7½ inches (19.1cm) below the upper ledger. Install flashing as needed to keep the house dry.

Build joist framing for the two sections on temporary supports. Because the decking runs diagonally, the joists should be 12 inches (30.5cm) apart rather than 16 inches (40.6cm). The framing sections are basic rectangles, but the lower level has a cutout for the stairway that is about 42 inches (1.1m) wide and 24 inches (61cm) deep. Attach the joists using joist hangers at the ledger, with screws or nails driven through the header joist at the front end.

Dig postholes for a straight row of footings parallel with the house. Position them so that the beams they support will not get in the way of the stairway stringers. Pour the concrete to a height 2 inches (5cm) or so above grade. Build the two beams from double 2x8s (5cmx20cm) or 2x10s 5cmx25cm), laminating the pieces with construction adhesive and a grid of nails or screws.

Hold each beam temporarily in place under the joists; then measure and cut posts to support the beam. Attach the posts and beams using the required framing hardware.

Cut stringers to reach a patio or concrete slab at the bottom. Install the stringers to the framing. Use decking pieces for the treads and 1x8s (2.5cmx20cm) for the risers.

DECKING. Cut a number of decking boards to 45 degrees at the ends that will abut the house. For each section, first install a long board near the middle; check it for straightness using a string line; and measure to be sure that it is at 45 degrees to the house. Then use decking spacers to install the other pieces, with ⅛-inch (0.3cm) gaps between boards. Wherever possible, allow boards to "run wild" past the end of the deck; then mark a row of them with a chalk line, and cut them all at once.

RAILING. Cut out the decking where the railing posts will go. Notch and install the posts using two lag screws driven into the framing. Two of the railing posts are about 10 feet (3m) tall to double as pergola posts.

To build the railing, cut 2x4 (5cmx10cm) top and bottom rails to fit between posts (keeping in mind the thickness of the railing brackets). Lay them out on the deck, and attach the balusters between them, spaced evenly, using the hardware that slips onto the balusters. Set each baluster section in place, and attach it using the railing brackets. Install railing cap made of decking carefully cut to form tight joints. Drill pilot holes, and drive screws in two or more directions to fasten the top cap securely.

PERGOLA. On a piece of cardboard the same width as the lumber pieces, use a compass or differently-sized round objects (a paint can, for instance) to trace the end-cut design for the pergola's beam and rafters. Mark the pieces, and cut them using a jigsaw.

Cut the tops of the pergola's posts level with each other. Cut and attach the two beam pieces on each side of the posts. Attach a ledger to the house for the pergola's rafters. (It does not need to be as strong as the deck's ledger.) Cut rafters to overhang the beam, and attach them, evenly spaced, using angle-driven screws. Cut and attach the top pieces, also evenly spaced, to the top of the rafters.

MATERIALS

» **FRAMING (ALL TREATED)**
- ❏ 4x4 (10cmx10cm) posts
- ❏ 2x8 (5cmx20cm) joists and ledgers
- ❏ Double 2x8s (5cmx20cm) for beams
- ❏ Joist hangers

» **FOOTINGS**
- ❏ Concrete

- ❏ Concrete tube forms
- ❏ Metal post anchors

» **DECKING AND FASCIA**
- ❏ 5/4x6 (3cmx15cm) cedar decking
- ❏ 1x8 (2.5cmx20cm) rough-face cedar for fascia

» **RAILING**
- ❏ 4x4 (10cmx10cm) cedar posts

- ❏ 2x4 (5cmx10cm) cedar top and bottom rails
- ❏ Metal balusters
- ❏ 5/4x6 (3cmx15cm) cedar decking for rail cap

» **PERGOLA (ALL CEDAR)**
- ❏ 4x4 (10cmx10cm) posts
- ❏ 2x8s (5cmx20cm) for ledger, beams, and rafters
- ❏ 2x2 (5cmx5cm) top pieces

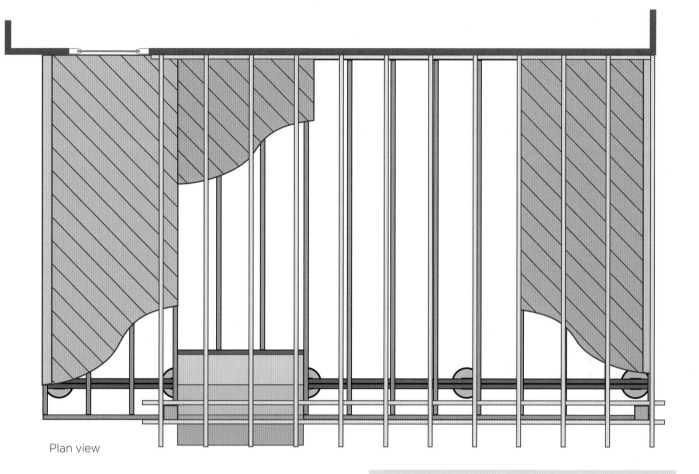

Plan view

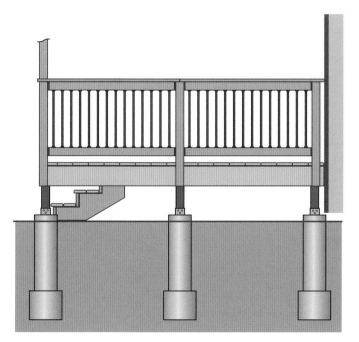

Elevation

Other Pergola Options

You can design an overhead ahead of time, or build the basic structure first, then experiment with the placement of top pieces afterward to adjust the shade to your liking. Of course, the closer together top pieces are spaced, the more shade. It is also true that 2x4s (5cmx10cm) laid on end (upright), as shown in the photo here, produce more shade when the sun is streaming at an angle, though they will not add much more shade than 2x2s (5cmx5cm) or 1x2s (2.5cmx5cm) when the sun is overhead.

Kitchen Counter Possibilities

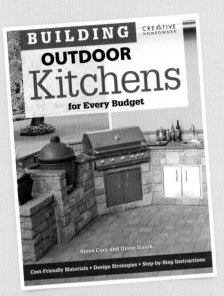

A variety of outdoor kitchen counters can be built on top of a deck. Lightweight faux masonry materials make it possible to build a counter that looks like solid stone but is amply supported by standard deck framing.

A counter's structure can be made of wood or steel studs, covered with concrete backer board, and then surfaced with faux stone, tile, or stucco. Or you can build cabinets out of PVC sheeting or hardwood. The countertop surface may be granite, quartz, tile, or even flagstone.

Like many deck builders these days, Boyer offers several types of outdoor kitchen counters. Here are some examples.

DIY outdoor kitchens. For full instructions on designing and building outdoor counters, see Creative Homeowner's *Building Outdoor Kitchens for Every Budget*. There you will find plenty of ideas for building cost-conscious counters that look great and provide durable service for many years. You will also find detailed step-by-step instructions for building a variety of counter types.

Simple granite counter. This simple but elegant counter has a straightforward frame made of ironwood 4x4s (10cmx10cm) and 2x4s (5cmx10cm) with granite slabs laid on top. A cart grill slips into an opening. The counter, at standard 36 inches (91cm) high, can double as a work surface or an eating table if you have chairs the right height.

Tile and granite counter. This counter is built using metal studs and concrete backer board (see above). The metal framing is lightweight but strong and fire-resistant, and the backer board will remain strong no matter what the weather brings. The backer board was then covered with slate tiles, and a granite slab top was installed (see at left). You can build wooden access doors or buy stainless-steel doors. Here, Joel used both and added a gas grill and a small sink. Other common options include a refrigerator or a side burner.

Built-in grill. Another approach is to frame the unit using treated 2x4s (2cmx10cm). In the example shown, the grill required a heat-protective metal sleeve, which is attached to the framing (see top right). (Some grills need this; others do not.) A set of wooden doors was added, and the backer board was covered with lightweight faux stone, which looks remarkably like the real thing (see bottom right). Finally, granite pieces were set on top, and the grill was installed (see above left).

Spacious Rooftop Getaway

Just above the bustle of the city, this half-enclosed rooftop deck, less than 20 steps from the house, offers diners and relaxers the option of shade or sun, as well as a private, comfortable place to unwind at the end of the day.

Lounging and dining. The overhead and trellis walls define a room that is part indoor and part outdoor. The two separate areas for diners and loungers are spacious but close enough together to permit friendly banter.

The Design

The owners of this urban rooftop deck rave about how much fresher and cleaner the air feels and how much quieter it seems on the deck. Yet it is only one and a half stories above the ground, so it is still possible to wave to the neighbors.

DINING AND LOUNGE AREA. The deck is built on a two-car, 20 x 21-foot (6.1m x 6.4m) garage with a flat roof. This makes for what is, by city standards, a wonderfully large outdoor room, the size of an indoor great room. The garage backs up onto an alley rather than a street, so auto and pedestrian traffic is limited.

One corner of the deck is nearly a full living room, with comfortable couches and a large coffee table. Nearby is the rectangular dining table for six. There's plenty of extra space in the unshaded part of the deck where lounging or reading chairs can be arranged. The portable grill can be placed here as well.

The owners bought a lightweight cart grill that can be carried up and down the stairs easily. They sometimes grill upstairs, so the cook can get in on the conversation with friends. At other times they prefer to place the grill on a lower landing just outside the kitchen.

LATTICE AND OVERHEAD. The latticework and the pergola are the most stunning features of this deck. The lattice panels, made of ½ x 1½-inch (1.3cm x 4cm) slats, are horizontally spaced 1 inch (2.5cm) apart, so the area that is covered is slightly greater than the area that is open. Still, because it is away from any foliage, plenty of light comes streaming in during the day.

The pergola features two massive 20-foot-long (6.1m) beams made from double pressure-treated 2x12s (5cmx30cm) wrapped with rough-sawn cedar 1-by (2.5cm-by) boards. The rafters are 2x10 (5cmx25cm) boards cut straight rather than with a decorative flourish to complement the geometric feel of the deck. The top pieces are 2x2s (5cmx5cm).

MATERIALS. Joel used ipé ironwood for the deck and stained it to a somewhat dark color. The pergola and lattice walls are all made of lighter-colored cedar, which seems to glow as it filters sunlight.

Lighting. Sconce lights with rectangular trim play off the geometric lines of the deck.

Access stairway. A simple stairway bump out gracefully leads to a landing below.

Kitchen access. The landing on the lower level, just outside the kitchen, houses a supply cabinet crafted from ironwood decking; the portable grill is often carried upstairs.

Building the Deck

Because the underlying garage roof may need to be repaired or replaced some day, the deck is built in framing sections that can be picked up if need be. Here, there are four framing sections, each about 10 x 10½ feet (3m x 3.2m).

THE GARAGE ROOF. Before building a rooftop deck, install a new rubber (EPDM or other material) roof, even if the existing roof is in reasonably good condition. If there are two or more layers of existing roofing (depending on local codes), you may need to tear off the old roof before installing the new one. The deck will partially protect the roof, but you should not expect even a new roof to last more than 20 years. From inside the garage, inspect the roof framing, and strengthen any joists that are cracked or otherwise damaged by fastening "sister" joists alongside them.

FRAMING. Each of the joist sections (or "pods") is attached to 4x4 (10cmx10cm) corner posts, which rest on top of 2x12 (5cmx30cm) boards, which in turn rest on thick neoprene sheets. (This is the material typically placed under air-conditioning units on a roof.) They are not actually attached to the roof; the weight of the deck holds them in place.

Build the joist sections with 2x8 (5cmx20cm) joists spaced every 16 inches (40.6cm) or 12 inches (30.5cm) if the decking will be run at an angle. Where the sections meet, the outside joists will be screwed together, creating a double joist.

A "flat" roof is usually slightly sloped. Start building the framing at the high end of the roof. Raise the sections onto temporary supports, checking that they are level in both directions. Once the sections are all level, fasten them together with screws where their joists run alongside each other.

You will install a post at each corner, which will mean that no joist will span a length more than 10 feet (3m).

At each post location, lay down a 14-inch-square (35.6cm) piece of ½-inch-thick (1.3cm) neoprene. On top of the neoprene, lay a 2x12 (5cmx30cm) that has been cut square. Position a short 4x4 (10cmx10cm) post on top of the 2x12 (5cmx30cm). Drive screws or nails through the joists into the post. Cut the post flush with the top of the joist. Repeat for all of the posts.

DECKING. Install the decking as you normally would, but use fasteners that can be removed later. Here, exposed square-head stainless-steel screws (color coated) are used. If possible, arrange the decking so quite a few of the pieces end with butt joints where the two joist sections meet. That will minimize the number of decking boards you will need to unscrew and remove if you need to pick up a section.

RAILING AND OVERHEAD. Attach the railing posts, and install railing as you would for a standard deck. Here, ipé components—4x4 posts (10cmx10cm), 2x4 (5cmx10cm) top and bottom rails, and 1x6 (2.5cmx15cm) top cap—are used with aluminum balusters.

For the overhead, attach tall 4x4 (10cmx10cm) posts every 4 feet (1.2m) to the sides of the deck, as you did with the railing posts. Attach beams made of two 2x12s (5cmx30cm) to span the long distance. Add 2x8 (5cmx20cm) joists, evenly spaced, and top with 2x2 (5cmx5cm) top pieces. To form walls, attach lattice panels to the outsides of the posts. Attach horizontal 2x4s (5cmx10cm) at the bottom, top, and halfway up the wall to cover the joints. Rip pieces of cedar to 1 inch (2.5cm) wide to use as trim to cover all of the exposed ends of the lattice.

MATERIALS

» **FRAMING (ALL TREATED)**
- ❑ 4x4 (10cmx10cm) posts
- ❑ 2x8 (5cmx20cm) joists
- ❑ 2x12 (5cmx30cm) stair stringers

» **FOOTINGS**
- ❑ 2x12 (5cmx30cm) short pieces
- ❑ ½ inch (1.3cm)-thick neoprene mats

» **DECKING AND FASCIA**
- ❑ 1x6 (2.5cmx15cm) ipé decking

» **RAILING**
- ❑ 4x4 (10cmx10cm) ipé posts
- ❑ 2x4 (5cmx10cm) ipé for top and bottom rails
- ❑ 1x6 (2.5cmx15cm) ipé decking for cap rail
- ❑ Powder-coated metal balusters

» **TRELLIS AND OVERHEAD (ALL CEDAR)**
- ❑ Trellis panels
- ❑ 2x12s (5cmx30cm) for beams
- ❑ 2x8 (5cmx20cm) rafters
- ❑ 2x2 (5cmx5cm) top pieces

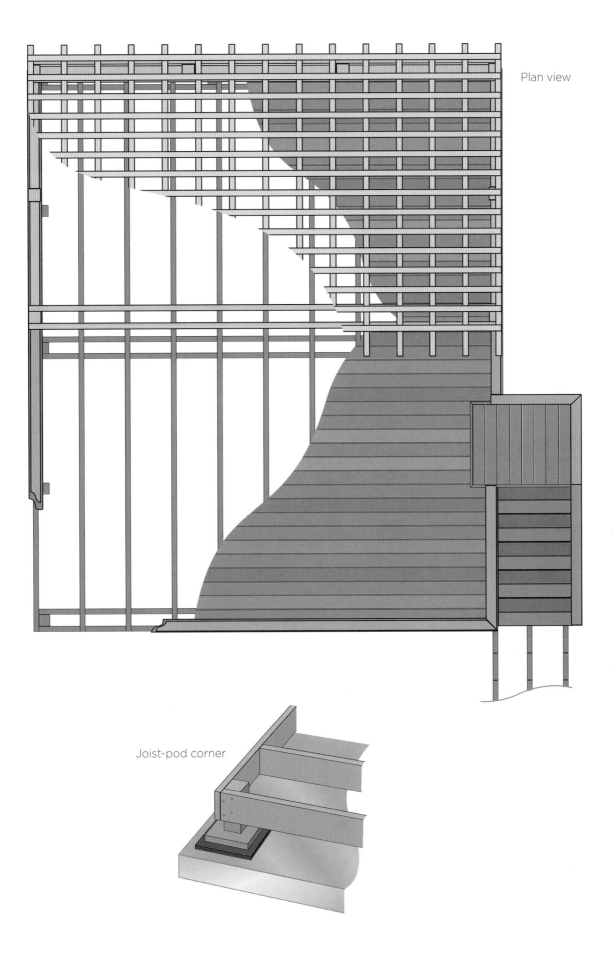

Plan view

Joist-pod corner

Versatile Family Room

A wide-open design with plenty of room for a variety of activities makes this deck feel like a large family room, with the addition of cooking and dining facilities.

The Design

The family wanted to generally increase their living space, with extra room for eating, relaxing, and cooking outdoors. This is accomplished with a single large platform—about 21 x 33 feet (6.4m x 10m) with an organic shape and a couple of built-in benches.

MODIFIED OCTAGON. Overall, the deck is a partial octagon with sides of uneven lengths. The angled stairway, indented into one of the sides, adds further complexity to the shape. The result is a deck with no two sides that are the same. This well-managed chaos makes perfect sense once use areas are defined, and the outer lines of the design contribute to a more interesting overall landscape.

Though the shape is open, individual "rooms" emerge once the furniture is in place. Near the counter, for instance, the adjoining space is perfect for a dining table and lounge chairs, with comfortable walking paths all around the table. The current round four-person table works, but a rectangular six-person table would fit as well.

MATERIALS. Nearly all of the visible parts are ipé. Once stained and sealed, some of the boards are darker than others, emphasizing the depth of the natural wood tones. The railing is also made of ipé, with gray metal balusters marching around the perimeter in pairs rather than individually.

STAIRWAY AND PATIO ENTRY. The wide four-step stairway opens out as it descends, for a gracious transition to the slate patio at the bottom. Natural stone always looks good next to natural wood; the fact that some of these stones display brownish tones that complement the wood colors helps unify the overall design within the landscape.

At the top of the stairway the railings are within 5 feet (1.5m) of each other, making it easy to install a pair of latching gates to keep the family's small dogs from escaping. Happy little dogs underfoot make this a friendly place for family relaxing and playing.

KITCHEN COUNTER. A simple but elegant kitchen counter at the perimeter of the deck makes it easy to prepare and cook food outdoors. The counter's granite slab top is supported by ipé framing and contains an open space below for storage.

Lounge chair seating. A pair of lounge chairs with a small end table between them is a classic arrangement. Potted flowers help tie things together on a deck; here they add definition and perk up the space with color.

Built-in bench. At the far end, a built-in bench anchors a separate seating area that faces the action on the other side of the deck; additional patio furniture can be added to suit the occasion.

Granite counter. This clean and simple design for an outdoor kitchen features a gleaming granite surface on each side of the grill at the right height for food preparation as well as for casual dining with stools. The beveled edge on the simple granite slab countertop adds a subtle touch of class.

Pet-friendly balusters. A distinctive railing made of ipé and pairs of square balusters keeps pets safely inside and lets the view show through.

Building the Deck

Use KDAT No. 1 treated lumber to ensure that the deck will stay firm and straight. You could install the footings, posts, and beams first, but building the framing on temporary supports and then installing the under supports makes it less likely that you will make mistakes in the footings. However, if digging is tough and you expect to hire a professional to machine-dig the postholes, you may choose to do the digging before you begin.

FRAMING. Install the ledger one deck board's thickness lower than the desired finish height of the deck. Attach flashing as needed to keep the house dry and direct water away from the ledger.

Build the joist framing on temporary supports. At the longest points, the joists must extend 21 feet (6.4m), which is too long for a normal 2x8 (5cmx20cm), so the joists will be "split" where the first beam will go. (See the plan view illustration on page 59.) Install a temporary support on each side of this future beam.

Attach joists to the ledger using joist hangers, and drive fasteners through header joists elsewhere. To frame the angled sections, install joists longer than they need to be. Make sure that they are evenly spaced; then use a chalk line or a straight board and pencil to mark them for cutting. Cut with a circular saw beveled at 45 degrees; then install the header board. Once the framing is complete, double the thickness of the header and outside joists by adding another 2x8 (5cmx20cm).

Dig postholes, and pour the footings, making sure they are in straight lines for the beams. Build the beams, and support them temporarily under the joists; then cut and attach posts to rest on the footings and support the beams.

STAIRS. The stair framing is fairly complicated. Five of the stringers are cut in the standard way. Two stringers on each side are shorter and must be cut at angles at their tops. The angled outside stringers are the most difficult. (You could install solid boards rather than notched stringers here, but then the treads and risers will need to be cut precisely at their ends.)

DECKING, RAILING, AND FINISH. Install the angled decking by first installing a long piece in the middle, checking to make sure it is straight and at 45 degrees to the house. Then install the other decking boards with small spaces between; check for straightness every four or five boards.

Notch the decking as needed to install the rail posts; then build baluster sections to fit between the posts. Top the railing with pieces of decking. At the corners, drill pilot holes and drive screws in several directions to ensure a long-lasting fit.

KITCHEN COUNTER. Hire a granite company to fabricate the countertop for you. Or consult Creative Homeowner's *Building Outdoor Kitchens for Every Budget* and cut the pieces yourself. Support the granite with simple framing made from 2x4s (5cmx10cm) and 4x4s (10cmx10cm).

MATERIALS

» **FRAMING (ALL TREATED)**
- ❑ 4x4 (10cmx10cm) posts
- ❑ 2x8s (5cmx20cm) for ledger and joists
- ❑ Double 2x8s (5cmx20cm) for beams
- ❑ 2x12 (5cmx30cm) stair stringers
- ❑ Joist hangers

» **FOOTINGS**
- ❑ Concrete
- ❑ Tube forms
- ❑ Metal post anchors

» **DECKING AND FASCIA**
- ❑ 1x6 (2.5cmx15cm) ipé decking

» **RAILING**
- ❑ 4x4 (10cmx10cm) ipé posts
- ❑ 2x4 (5cmx10cm) ipé for top and bottom rails
- ❑ 1x6 (2.5cmx15cm) ipé decking for cap rail
- ❑ Powder-coated metal balusters

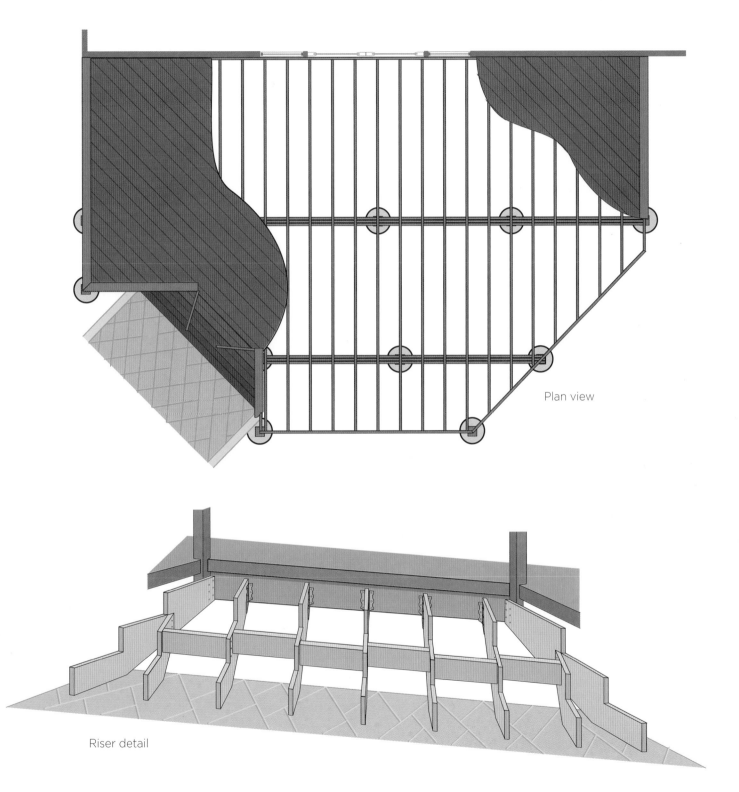

Plan view

Riser detail

Private City Loft

Even a single-car garage with a flat roof can offer enough room to build a deck that is big enough for intimate—or even medium-size—gatherings.

The Design

The garage that supports this deck is only 14 feet (4.3m) wide and 21 feet (6.4m) long—enough room for a modestly sized deck. The garage is 10 feet (3m) from the house, so there is also a small lower deck spanning between the garage and the house. You leave the house to step onto the lower stairway, then walk up a set of stairs to reach the upper deck.

COZY BOWER. The owners do not do heavy-duty grilling here, though there is room for a small barbecue on either level. The deck is raised about 16 feet (4.9m) aboveground, creating a pleasant tree-house effect.

Lattice walls that run about two-thirds of the way around the deck provide privacy and a nice sense of enclosure. A large overhanging tree on the side that is wall-free provides a leafy backdrop that also feels partially enclosed. A sectional couch anchors the comfortable "living room" space with walls on all three sides. The adjacent "dining room," in a more open-air space, seems nestled in the tree's branches.

PERGOLA. The 7-foot-tall (2.1m) overhead structure provides only minimal shade, mostly acting as a visual frame. It is made of double beams running in a grid of sections that are about 4 x 6 feet (1.2m x 1.8m). The effect is cleanly geometric without feeling overly formal.

MATERIALS AND FINISH. The decking is a composite in a gray color but with a slight faux wood grain. The other components are wood, covered with a solid stain that closely matches the decking. A putty color like this, while certainly not a natural wood tone, nonetheless has a natural feel reminiscent of old boards that have weathered.

Lower deck.
The lower deck functions as an out-of-the-way place for the garbage and a pseudo-foyer to bridge the transition between the upper deck, the house, and the yard.

Personalized accessories. The neutral gray color is a pleasant serene backdrop that is fun to accessorize. Plants and other personal touches add cheerful splashes of color.

Dining area. Just the right amount of sunlight filters through the tree onto the dining table. The open section of the deck permits a pleasant view of the neighborhood yet preserves a sense of privacy, so diners do not feel they are on display.

Practical fascia. At the garage's eave, fascia disguises the roof's slope, which is not parallel with the deck.

Simple cooling. The outdoor-rated ceiling fan keeps things cool. Its blades were painted to blend with the surroundings.

TRELLIS AND RAILING. Painted 4x4 (10cmx10cm) posts support the railing and the trellis walls. The trellis panels are cedar, in a "Moderna" pattern that features narrow horizontal slits that filter out most of the light while leaving the surrounding cityscape visible in a dreamy sort of way. Simple squared-off trim pieces attach the lattice to the posts; they also decorate the joint between the walls and the pergola beams. This slightly softens the geometric look, and adds visual texture.

LOWER DECK. About ten steps down from the garage-top deck, the small lower deck makes good use of its small space. A built-in couch is secluded but at the same time is within easy speaking range of guests upstairs or playing children in the yard below.

Building the Deck

The framing is made in separate sections, or "pods," that can be removed if need be to repair the roof. The railing and pergola posts are attached to the outside of the framing. In this case, the existing gable roof was removed and a flat roof installed to accommodate the deck.

FRAMING AND DECKING. For instructions on building in sections, setting the sections on neoprene pads, and installing decking, see the Spacious Rooftop Getaway deck (pages 52–55). For this deck, there are three sections, each about 7 x 13 feet (2.1m x 4m), with 6x6 (15cmx15cm) corner posts and no 2x12 (5cmx30cm) pads.

For the lower deck, attach and flash ledgers to both the house and the garage. Use joist hangers at both ends to run the joists. Codes may require you to install a beam as well.

PERGOLA AND RAILING. Notch the decking as needed to attach the posts to the outside joists. Notch and attach the posts—7 to 8 feet (2.1m to 2.5m) high for the pergola and 3 feet (91cm) high or as required by code for the railing—using lag bolts.

Cut and attach the 2x8 (5cmx20cm) beam pieces—one on each side of each post—running perpendicular to the length of the deck. Cut 2x8s (5cmx20cm) to fit between, running in the other direction. This includes 3½ inch (8.9cm)-long pieces between the double beam pieces.

For the trellis, install horizontal 2x4s (5cmx10cm) between the posts to make frames for the lattice panels. Make trim pieces by rip-cutting pieces of 2-by (5cm-by) lumber to an inch (2.5cm) thick or so. Cut trellis panels to fit, and sandwich them between trim pieces that are attached to the posts and the horizontal 2x4s (5cmx10cm). To make the railing, cut 2x4 (5cmx10cm) top rails (which are also the rail cap) to span the length of the railing and 2x4 (5cmx10cm) bottom rails to fit between the posts. Cut a series of 2x2 (5cmx5cm) balusters. Lay the rails on the deck, and measure and mark for evenly spaced balusters. Attach the balusters by driving screws through the rails. Place the baluster sections on the posts, and use screws to attach them.

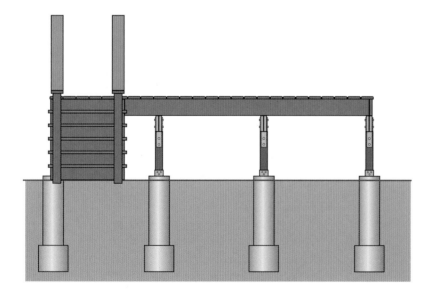

Elevation

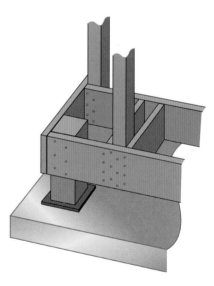

Joist-pod corner
with posts

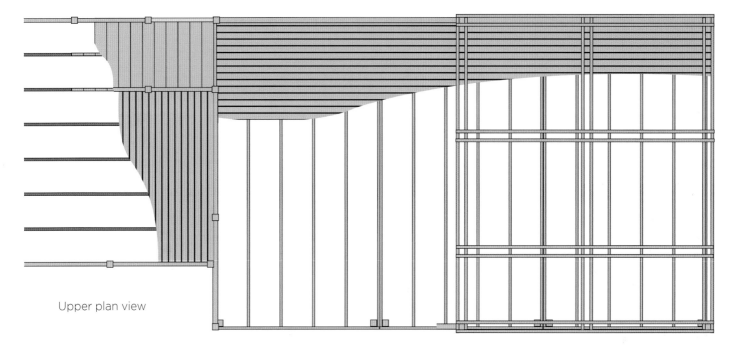

Upper plan view

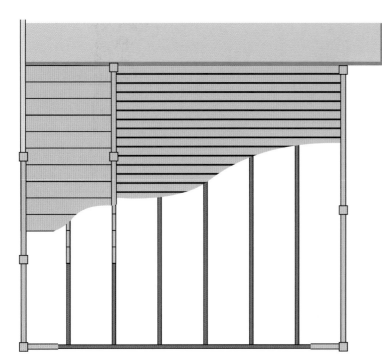

Lower plan view

MATERIALS

» **FRAMING (ALL TREATED)**
- ❏ 6x6 (15cmx15cm) posts
- ❏ 2x8 (5cmx20cm) joists and ledgers
- ❏ 2x12 (5cmx30cm) stair stringers

» **FOOTINGS**
- ❏ ½ inch (1.3cm)-thick neoprene mats

» **DECKING AND FASCIA**
- ❏ 5/4x6 (3cmx15cm) composite decking
- ❏ ½ inch (1.3cm) fascia board
- ❏ Aluminum eave and gutter material

» **RAILING, WALLS, OVERHEAD**
- ❏ 4x4 (10cmx10cm) treated posts
- ❏ 2x4 (5cmx10cm) treated for top and bottom rails
- ❏ 2x2 (5cmx5cm) treated balusters
- ❏ Cedar trellis panels
- ❏ Trim pieces ripped from treated 2-bys (5cm-bys)
- ❏ 2x12s (5cmx30cm) treated for beams
- ❏ Lag bolts

BUILDER PROFILE:
Decks, Inc.

Ivan Arana builds decks in Maryland, Virginia, and the Washington, D. C., area. He often works in conjunction with Clemens Jellema of Fine Decks, Inc. (featured in the third edition of *Deck Designs*). Ivan is actually licensed as a medical doctor in Peru, his country of origin, but has chosen to make a life in the U. S. as a designer and builder.

Most of his clients are discriminating customers who want a finely crafted outdoor space that is both a showcase and a pleasure to use. His decks are carefully designed with an eye toward balancing symmetry and proportion and achieving harmony with the surroundings.

Thoughtful design. An overhead made with translucent panels partially covers a lower deck and houses an overhead fan for summertime heat relief. Cable railings and expertly installed ipé stairs, posts, and decking create a pleasantly textured feel for the space.

Ivan Arana
DECKS, INC.
Owings, MD
301-789-7447
www.finedecks.com

HIS DESIGNS

Arana is a fearless builder, and virtually all design options are on the table. His decks often feature multiple curves, which some builders shy away from. Decking patterns may be simple or elaborate, with boards meeting at odd angles or curved pieces set in the middle for an inlaid floor effect. Creative possibilities for railings and pergolas cover a range of styles, from a simple rustic cabin look to fanciful columns and overhead outrigger pieces.

He believes that a deck should not overpower the house, so he advises against building one that occupies more than 80 percent of a house's back wall. On a large house his decks are often 500 square feet (46.5m²) or more, but on medium-size or small houses he urges people to buy smaller decks to achieve the right proportion.

Though his decks may look like works of art, they are also sized and shaped to accommodate ample space for cooking, dining, and lounging, with pathways between and around use areas. When the deck has stairs leading to the lawn, Arana makes sure there is a clear path from the kitchen door to the stairs. (After all, even upper-class customers need to take the garbage out.)

FINISH MATERIALS

Arana's clients want surfaces that stay clean looking without much maintenance. For that reason, composite finish materials are the rule rather than the exception on his decks. Most of his decking and fascia is made with high-end composite materials that have a proven record of durability—so they retain their original appearance decades later. Many of these composites have realistic-looking faux wood grain; from a distance, people often mistake them for real wood.

For parts of the deck that will be handled or looked at up close—such as the top cap of a railing, a bench, or planters—Arana often uses ipé or other Brazilian hardwood. Many people prefer the natural beauty of real wood where detail woodworking is on display. The drawback is that wood requires yearly cleaning and sealing, but for a small area the task is quite manageable.

Handrail joints. A top rail and handrail show off Arana's perfect joinery. Screw heads are hidden beneath wood plugs.

Overhead options. This heroic-looking pergola is made of low-maintenance vinyl.

Quality work. A lower-priced deck made with pressure-treated decking gains lots of style points if it is judiciously stained and finished regularly.

Strong framing. Extra-beefy framing makes for an extra-strong deck. Here, there is plenty of support for decking run in two directions.

Special touches. This hardwood planter/bench combo showcases the advantage of using wood for visible details. The lighter shade of wood complements the slightly darker composite flooring.

Unique porches. Arana also builds screened porches. This one features an expansive open section, made possible by the use of super-strong screening.

Craftsman decking. Decking pieces with a geometric inlay design show off Arana's fine craftsmanship.

Dining options. A two-level granite counter surface is a simple add-on feature that doesn't take up much space but can be used as an eating bar, a food-preparation area, or a buffet surface for food and drink. Diners at this counter can keep the chef company.

CRAFTSMANSHIP

An occasional gap or imperfect joints on a deck may not bother many people, but quality workmanship brings a deck to the next level. Arana's exacting standards shine through in the details of his decking, railing, benches, and other features, which have neat and consistently tight joints. This high level of craftsmanship comes from years of experience developing carpentry skills—and from the use of quality finish materials that will avoid warping or shrinkage. A rock-solid underlying structure is also critical to ensure that joints will stay tight for a long time.

On railings and other woodworking-intense features, Arana often sinks screws below the surface and fills holes with wood plugs so that you see exposed dowels rather than fastener heads; the result is a finished Craftsman-style appearance.

Arana almost always installs decking with hidden fasteners so that there are no exposed screw or nail heads.

Many composites come with their own hidden fastener systems. For wood decking, he uses fasteners with a proven track record.

Many decks are built with decking that simply overhangs the perimeter. Arana—again, for a more finished, furniture-like appearance—often installs perimeter "picture frames," which may be made from the same material as the decking or may be in a contrasting color.

Many decks have butt joints—places where two pieces of decking meet end to end. These joints are unsightly and can be problem spots in the future. For a cleaner appearance, Arana designs and builds to avoid these joints. That may mean installing decking that runs in several different directions or adding an inlaid strip in the middle of a large area.

Hiring a Good Builder for an Inexpensive Deck

If you are looking for someone to build a reasonably priced deck, you may think that someone like Arana would be out of your price range. But he is happy to build modest decks and will no doubt do a better job than many low-end builders. And you may be pleasantly surprised by his price.

Arana will likely propose a deck with a bit of flair rather than a plain rectangle—perhaps a couple of angled corners or a railing with some attractive details. For a typical pressure-treated deck he often charges about $25 per square foot (0.09m²), which means that, for instance, a 12 x 16-foot (3.7m x 4.9m) deck would cost about $4,800. If you want ipé or composite, the cost would jump to about $45 per square foot (0.09m²).

Arana's Techniques

1 To ensure that the deck's structure will not move, Arana builds with No. 1 pressure-treated lumber or kiln-dried after treatment (KDAT) lumber. Joists, posts, and beams made from less-expensive material will warp and shrink over time, which often will make the finish materials move slightly and put joinery out of whack.

2 He uses 6x6 (15cmx15cm) structural posts even where 4x4s (10cmx10cm) would pass code. Also, Arana's beams are all double 2x10s (5cmx25cm) or 2x12s (5cmx30cm), even if 2x8s (5cmx20cm) would meet code. This "overbuilding" ensures solidity.

3 Arana installs most of his joists 12 inches (30.5cm) apart, even when 16-inch (40.6cm) spacing would be allowed. Also, he doubles the perimeter joists, which makes for a firmer surface for attaching the railing posts—so his railings rarely wobble.

4 If siding must be cut out to install a ledger, Arana takes extra care to ensure against water infiltration by installing two pieces of flashing—one flat piece against the wall and behind the ledger, and another, angled, piece that goes over the ledger. He prefers vinyl flashing to metal.

5 Even if there is a ledger, Arana usually installs a beam with posts near the house for extra strength.

6 Because Arana raises many of his decks 8 feet (2.5m) or taller, he takes special care to choose posts that are straight and made of kiln-dried wood because they will show.

7 Though Arana sometimes paints framing pieces that will be visible, he often wraps them with vinyl fascia material.

8 Where he builds an upper-level deck and wants to keep the area below dry, Arana installs his own drainage system, which uses rubber material thicker than what is usually used. (See pages 92–93.)

Well Rounded

With its fan-shaped main level, and a spa area down a few steps, this finely crafted deck is perfectly suited to its woodsy setting.

The Design

The practical goals here were to provide space for lounging, cooking, and dining, as well as a partially secluded spa area. Just as important were aesthetic goals: creating a deck that was stunning and serene.

MEETING SEVERAL GOALS. The owners wanted a pleasant place to relax and enjoy their forest setting, and they were looking for a deck that made a splashy design statement. They also wanted to add a spa with ample seating—and they wanted the spa to be convenient but out of sight from the street. Their existing square-ish deck was disappointing on all these counts; the new deck meets all the goals head on.

Sometimes it takes the combined efforts of an architect, a builder, and the customers to get things just right. The owners initially worked with an architect who, they felt, came up with some good ideas, but did not produce an overall design that resonated with them. They turned to Ivan, whose extensive deck-building experience helped hammer out the final design.

THE MAIN DECK. The upper level features a gentle curve in front, which not only looks great, but also helps provide suitable space for the round dining table. The outer curve is mimicked by a curved decking inlay piece facing the opposite direction with the same curve profile. This provides a sense of partial symmetry that makes the deck feel casual and luxurious at the same time.

The decking is composite material with a natural-looking wood grain pattern. The curved inlaid decking piece solves a problem: without it, some of the decking runs would be more than 20 feet (6.1m). Because decking boards longer than 20 feet (6.1m) are not available, that would mean end-to-end decking butt joints, which are less than desirable. Typical of Arana's decks, a darker trim board runs around the perimeter, forming a frame of sorts.

Casual seating. Just outside the house door is a great spot to relax yet still be close to the action in the kitchen or on the deck. Sometimes a good view is facing where the people are.

Finishing details. Arana sinks his rail cap screws, then squirts a bit of polyurethane glue in the holes and presses in wood plugs, which he makes himself out of ipé. After the glue has dried, he sands the plugs smooth.

Shade options. This kind of portable umbrella gracefully reaches over from the side to provide shade, requiring no hole in the middle of the table.

RAILING. Arana has made the railing of ipé with metal balusters. He covers the screws, attaching the upper rail to the top cap with plugs for a neat appearance.

Although the deck edge is curved, the railing along the edge does not curve but instead makes a series of tiny turns. Installing a curved railing is difficult and expensive if you use hardwood, and Arana felt that the straight boards actually made for a more interesting look.

THE SPA DECK. The spa is situated just barely out of sight of neighbors and passersby, yet still with easy access with the main deck and the house. The spa's upper rim is just one step down from the main deck, and its surrounding deck is just two steps down.

Getting into and out of a spa is easier on some decks. For instance, spas that rest on top of the deck have a rim about 3 feet (91cm) high, requiring a small set of two steps for entering and exiting the water. If the spa is situated at a lower level so that its rim is just barely above the deck, bathers may need to crouch to get in and out. Here, the rim is about 17 inches (43.2cm) above the deck, which may be the most graceful arrangement.

Because the spa is adjacent to a section of railing, the cover can tilt up against the railing to form a short privacy wall when opened. The built-in benches in front of the spa are finished with composite decking, which is impervious to water. The wide stairs leading down to the spa deck are often used as seating areas as well.

Simple lighting. Low-voltage lighting on the step risers and railing posts, as well as inside the spa, make this a magical spot at night.

Craftsman joinery. Quality joinery is a thing of beauty. This combination of picture-frame pieces and inlay creates a beautiful pattern that requires precision cutting.

Unique fascia. Skirting made from decking boards is neatly finished with a rip-cut piece of 1-by (2.5cm-by) ipé at the bottom; a vinyl fascia board fits between the railing posts.

Building the Deck

Building a deck with curves—especially when using composite lumber—calls for specialized skills and is a job that may be best left to professionals. The many visible joints in the deck and railing also call for top-notch carpentry skills.

FRAMING. Use high-quality No. 1 or KDAT lumber. Attach the ledger along both sides of the house, about 2½ inches (6.5cm) below the threshold. Install flashing as needed to keep the house and the ledger dry.

Build the framing for the upper level, with joists 12 inches (30.5cm) apart, on temporary supports. Allow the joists to run long where the curve will be. Tack a board on top to ensure that the joists are correctly spaced; then use a straight board or chalk line to mark for cutting their ends. As shown in the drawing, the header joist does not need to be curved; straight pieces with gentle angles will work fine. After cutting the joists, install the header.

Frame the lower spa level 15 inches (38.1cm) below the upper level [or in increments of 7½ inches (19.1cm), depending on how many steps there will be]. Consult with the spa's literature to ensure that you leave enough room for it.

After the levels are framed, temporarily hang the beams under the joists. Dig postholes and suspend posts in the holes, following codes. Pour concrete as needed, and backfill the holes, again following codes.

SLAB FOR THE SPA. Consult the spa manufacturer's literature and dig a hole as needed for the spa's supporting slab. Most slabs are at least 6 inches (15.2cm) deep. You may need to build forms out of 2-bys (5cm-bys) if the slab rises above the ground. Tamp the soil firm, pour half of the concrete, and embed metal reinforcement as required by code. Pour the rest of the concrete.

DECKING AND STAIRS. Lay decking at a 45-degree angle to the house. For installing a border and a center inlaid piece, see pages 80–81.

For the entry stairs, set rail posts at the bottom in concrete. Pour or lay a small slab or patio to support the bottoms of the stringers. Cut the stringers; attach them at the top using joist hangers; and anchor them to the bottom. Install treads made of two decking boards and risers made of vinyl fascia.

RAILING. Notch the decking as needed, and bolt the railing posts. Cut 2x4 (5cmx10cm) top and bottom rails to fit between the posts, and use the railing system's brackets to fasten them. At the curved section, these pieces must be cut at a slight bevel.

If you will add railing lights, cut a groove in the back of the posts, and drill holes for the lights. Run the wiring; then cover the post backs with 1x4s (2.5x10cm).

The decorative metal balusters simply screw to the face of the top and bottom rails.

MATERIALS

» **FRAMING (ALL TREATED)**
- ❑ 6x6 (15cmx15cm) posts
- ❑ 2x8s (5cmx20cm) for ledger and joists
- ❑ Double 2x8s (5cmx20cm) for beams
- ❑ 2x8s (5cmx20cm) for stair framing
- ❑ Joist hangers

» **FOOTINGS**
- ❑ Concrete for post footings
- ❑ Concrete and metal reinforcement for slab under the spa

» **DECKING AND FASCIA**
- ❑ 5/4x6 (3cmx15cm) composite decking
- ❑ Vinyl fascia material

» **RAILING**
- ❑ 4x4 (10cmx10cm) ipé posts
- ❑ 2x4 (5cmx10cm) ipé for top and bottom rails
- ❑ 5/4x6 (3cmx15cm) ipé decking for cap rail
- ❑ Powder-coated metal balusters

» **PLANTER/BENCH**
- ❑ Treated 2x4s (5cmx10cm) and 2x6s (5cmx15cm) for framing
- ❑ Treated 4x6s (10cmx15cm) or double 2x6s (5cmx15cm) for uprights
- ❑ Decking boards to cover

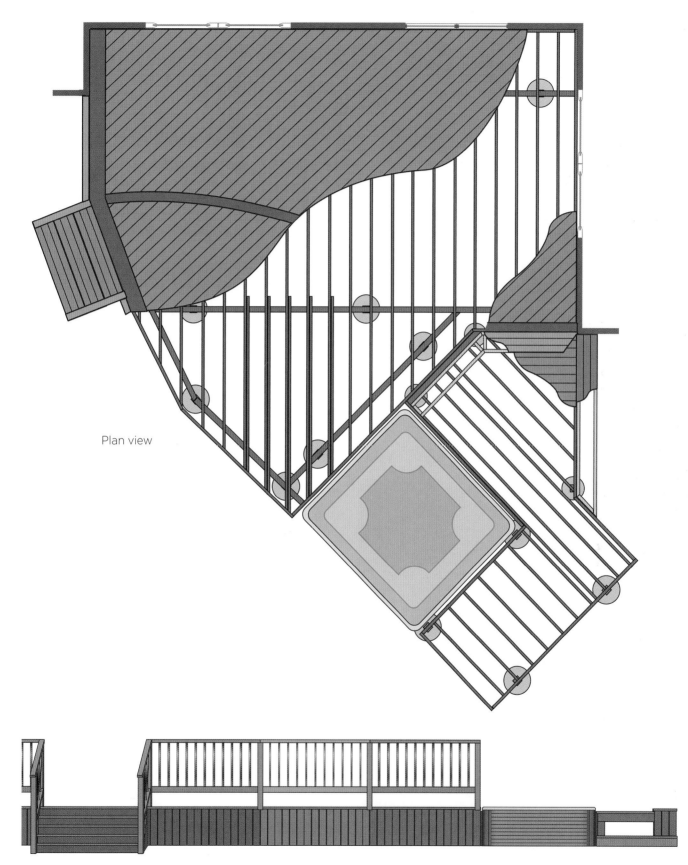

Plan view

Elevation

Quality Techniques

The next four pages show some of Arana's more-advanced building techniques. Some are within reach of a do-it-yourselfer; others are clearly for skilled and experienced professionals. Whether you will build yourself or hire a contractor, knowing about these methods can help ensure that your deck will be stronger and better looking.

SOME FANCY DECKING. Decking inlays and borders like this are recommended only for very skilled carpenters, since all the cuts must be made perfectly.

Use a measuring tape and pencil as a large compass to mark where the curve will be on top of the deck framing. Install blocking as needed so that all the decking boards will be supported at their ends. Install the decking boards so they butt up against the marks.

Bend the composite decking boards to the correct curve. This is often done using special equipment, such as a heating "blanket" made for the purpose. In this case, Arana was working on an extremely hot day and laid the boards out on a dark asphalt surface. Once they got hot enough, he bent and pressed the boards against pieces of plywood that he had cut at the correct curve. He clamped them in position and left them for two days.

Place the curved board on the deck where it will go, and weight it so it will not move. Using the curved board as a template, mark the decking for cutting. Use a circular saw to cut the lines. A standard circular saw blade will work for gentle curves, but if you have a tight curve, use a special curve-cutting blade. Of course, these cuts must be exceptionally accurate.

Set the curved board in the cutout, and mark its ends for cutting to length, if needed. Drive small-headed screws to fasten the inlay piece.

The photo on the bottom right of page 81 shows installing the curved border piece. If it is even slightly out of alignment, two or more helpers with pry bars will be needed to bend it into place while it is being fastened.

Mark the curved inlay. After heating and curving the requisite boards, lay them in place and use them as templates to mark the decking for cutting.

Cut for the curved inlay. Following the pencil marks made using the curved boards as templates, carefully cut the decking with a circular saw.

Attach the inlay boards. Lay the curved boards in the cutouts; cut them to length at the ends, and drive long small-headed screws to secure them.

Install curved border pieces. Although the border boards have been heated and curved, they may still need some additional hands to persuade them into place.

BOX FRAMING FOR STEPS.

For long steps between decking levels, it is often impractical to frame using stair stringers. Instead, build boxes of 2x8s (5cmx20cm). Rip-cut the pieces for the bottom box to lower it by one decking board's thickness. Build the boxes with crosspieces at least every 16 inches (40.6cm). Fasten the boxes; then install decking and then fascia.

Stair platforms. Make platforms instead of saw-tooth stringers for long steps on a deck. Reduce the height of the first platform by the thickness of a decking board.

Platform framing. Here the top deck is three steps up from the lower deck. Using 2x8 (5cmx20cm) framing makes sense because the 7¾-inch (19.7cm) width makes a good riser.

Bench framing. Using a finished height of 17 inches (43.2cm) and a width of three decking boards minus the thickness of two boards and 2 inches (5cm), frame the bench using 2x6s (5cmx15cm).

BUILDING A PLANTER/BENCH.

Build a tall planter by constructing a frame of treated 2x4s (5cmx10cm), then covering its sides with good-looking wood or composite decking. You can add a ledge inside the frame to hold plastic flowerpots, or have a metal fabricator make a galvanized insert for holding soil.

To make a bench that attaches, build another frame out of 2x6s (5cmx15cm), with crosspieces every 16 inches (40.6cm) or so. The width of the bench framing should be equivalent to the width of three decking boards minus the thickness of two decking boards, minus 2 inches (5cm) for overhang. Use 4x6s (10cmx15cm), as shown, or double 2x6s (5cmx15cm) for upright supports. A standard bench height is 17 inches (43.2cm). Attach the 2x6 (5cmx15cm) framing to the uprights and to the planter; then cover it with decking.

RAILING POST. Composite decking systems often call for installing posts inside the framing, before the decking is laid. Wood posts, like the one shown here, are most often installed outside the framing, after the decking is installed and before the fascia. Some deck builders notch 4x4 (10cmx10cm) railing posts at the bottom so that they feel more like part of the deck. But many builders, like Arana, do not notch because they feel that it weakens the post. Determine the post's location, and notch the decking so that the post can snug up tight to the outside joist. Prepare the post by drilling pilot holes; then countersink holes for ½-inch-diameter (1.3cm) lag screws; a 6-inch (15.2cm) screw will go through the post and most of the way through a doubled outside joist. In this case, a groove was also added to discreetly run electrical cable for a post light. Have a helper hold the post plumb in both directions; drill pilot holes into the joists; and use a drill-driver to drive the lag screws.

Notch the decking. After determining where you will place the railing posts, use a portable jigsaw to notch (the thickness of the overhang) the outside pieces of decking at those locations.

Install the posts. Drill holes for two lag screws in each post as shown. (See text.) If needed for an electrical cable, cut a groove in the outside surface of the posts using a router.

Post-light wiring. Drill a hole that is wide enough to accommodate the light wiring, and thread the wiring as shown. The wire runs in the groove you previously cut into the post. Cover the groove with trim.

Post-light installation. Split the wire; strip a few inches of insulation; and attach the wire to the base plate of the light. Attach the plate to the post, and finish installing the rest of the light.

POST LIGHT. To install a post light, drill a hole through the post and into the groove in the back of the post. Run the cable through the groove, and pull the cable through the hole. Strip the insulation, and attach the wiring to the light; then attach the rail light. Cover the post's groove with a 1x4 (2.5cmx10cm) board.

ATTACHING RAILS. Many top and bottom rails are attached using angle-driven screws or nails, but this method is not reliable—and rails may come loose in a few years. Instead, buy rail brackets. Attach the brackets to the rail; then position the rail, and drive screws through the bracket to attach the rail to the post.

Attach a bracket to the rail. Using brackets is a more secure way than toenailing (or fastening angled screws) to attach rails to railing posts on a deck. The first step is to attach the bracket as shown.

Attach the rail to the post. Once you have attached the brackets, secure the rails to the posts. For this railing, the rail is attached flush to the top of the post.

STAIR RAILING POSTS. The railing posts at the bottom of a set of stairs are sometimes wobbly. That is because many builders use posts that reach just down to the ground and simply attach them to the sides of the stringers. Here is a better method: after framing the stairs, dig postholes 36 inches (91cm) or deeper next to the bottom of the stringers on each side. Add a second piece of 2-by (5cm-by) lumber to the inside of the stringer. Set the post in the hole; hold it plumb; drill holes; and fasten with long bolts. Fill the hole with concrete, and you will have a bottom post that will not wiggle.

Wobble-proof bottom post. For rock-steady railing posts at the bottom of deck stairs, frame the stairs and then dig postholes on each side next to the bottom of the stringers as shown.

Fasten the posts. Double up the stringer lumber at the bottom; then drill for and fasten carriage bolts to a plumbed-up post as shown. Fill the posthole with concrete.

PLUGGING AND SINKING. Arana countersinks his rail cap screws, then squirts a bit of polyurethane glue in the holes and presses in wood plugs, which he makes himself out of ipé. After the glue has dried, he sands the plugs smooth. He also takes the time to sand corners and edges, so there will be no splinters.

Now you see it. When you need to use screws on visible surfaces, countersink them. Using plugs the same diameter as the hole made from the same wood, insert glue-covered plugs as shown.

Now you don't. When the glue on the plugs has dried, sand the wood surface using a belt or pad sander with medium to light sanding grit. The plugs will blend in with the surrounding wood.

Smooth to the touch. To avoid splinters on unpainted wooden deck railings, run a belt sander with light sanding grit along the edges and corners of the railing cap as shown.

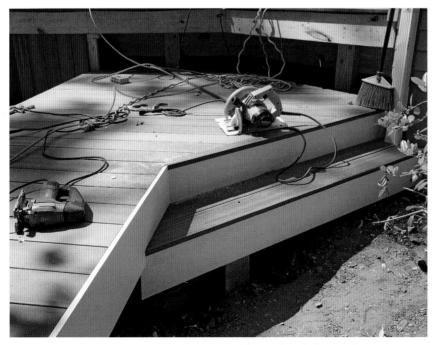

Step overhangs. Where a deck has been designed with fascia that comes flush with the top of the decking, you should treat steps differently. Overhang the step decking by ½ inch (1.25cm) past the fascia.

TWO FASCIA ARRANGEMENTS. Around the perimeter of the deck, Arana often cuts the decking boards perfectly flush with the outside joists, then installs fascia boards with their top edges flush with the decking surface. (You can see this arrangement in the left portion of the photo.) But on steps, that configuration would cause problems, because people would step on the narrow, white fascia. On the step shown, he overhangs the decking by the thickness of the fascia, plus ½ inch (1.3cm). On the deck itself, he installs a one-half-wide border piece, which also overhangs the fascia by ½ inch (1.3cm).

85

Expansive Balcony

Outside a second-story kitchen door, this deck is oriented toward the view. It is not spacious in terms of square feet, but its length accommodates a variety of use areas.

The Design

This home's property slopes down to the water's edge, and the back door on the main level is one story up from the ground. The solution: an elevated deck. A long deck like this makes the most of the sweeping view, which is stunning from any point along the deck.

SHAPE AND SIZE. For almost one-half of its length, the deck is only 10 feet (3m) wide, which is fairly narrow by high-end deck standards. But it is ample room for a set of chairs with a small table, plus a pathway. It is long enough so that the owners can place one set of chairs facing out and one facing toward the house. Ten feet (3m) is also wide enough for a modest grilling area, which the owners placed at the far end.

A slightly longer section is 16 feet (4.9m) wide. Here, a sheltered dining area occupies a 10 x 12-foot (3m x 3.7m) space at the corner of the deck, oriented for maximum view enjoyment. The area behind the dining table provides space for traffic and food supply. An open space to the side of the dining area, about 12 x 16 feet (3.7m x 4.9m), serves multiple purposes. For now, the owners have placed furniture for a conversation area, but lounge chairs with end tables or even a hammock or two would also work well here.

DECKING AND RAILING. The neutral-color composite decking does not try to imitate natural wood but still has a natural feel. The putty and tan tones form a pleasant mellow backdrop for colorful personal touches—bright yellow flowers and green foliage, splashy dinnerware, striped cushions, and platters of fruit and vegetables.

The cable railing has ten horizontal cables, which are so thin they barely affect the view. The posts and rails are slightly darker than the decking, and the row of red caps on the posts (which cover adjusting nuts for the cables) adds whimsical detail.

Beautiful light. A deck is a great spot to enjoy shifting patterns of light as the sun begins to set. Here the table looks like a still life from a classic work of art.

Simple seating. In a sunny spot on the deck, a cozy seating area is the perfect place to unwind with a book and a cup of tea.

Out-of-the-way grilling. At the far end of the deck, the grill's smoke will not bother others. And the potted yellow flowers in bloom bring garden charm to the deck.

THE OVERHEAD. Sheltered by a "Santa Fe" style vinyl pergola, the dining area is well protected. Rather than having a large number of closely-spaced rafters with decorative end cuts, it features only two beams and three upper pieces, all massively sized and with end profiles that are much like post caps. The vinyl posts were sanded and painted to match the decking.

The pergola has a canvas canopy that is retractable on top and on the sides. This was expensive, but it keeps diners comfortable no matter where the sun is. When choosing a canopy or awning, it is usually worth it to pay extra for a unit that can be easily moved up and down or from side to side because it means you can use the space more often. This model is simple and straightforward, with awnings that slide to the side and shades that pull up and down using chains, but you can also choose mechanisms with cranks or even motorized units.

Enjoying the view. To the left of the dining table is a conversation pit, oriented toward the view.

Blocking. Near the house, blocking installed between the joists provides an ample fastening surface for the picture-frame decking border and the ends of the decking boards.

Lighting. When the sun goes down and soft lights begin to glow, a deck can be a magical place.

Unique posts and railings. The cable railing system features caps on the posts that can be removed to tighten the cables—something you may need to do several times in the first few years.

LIGHTING AND FAN. The lights are standard voltage (rather than low-voltage) and are controlled by dimmers just inside the door. Each railing post has a downward-facing round light; the pergola posts have sconces that point up and down. An outdoor-rated ceiling fan/light provides ambient illumination. A high-quality fan (one that does not make much noise and has large blades) can make a difference on hot, humid days.

ON THE GROUND. The long structural posts and beams were carefully chosen for straightness and were covered with a solid stain custom-tinted to match the decking. The joists are not painted because they are not highly visible.

Building the Deck

Building an upper-story deck is a challenging project, so tackle it only if you are experienced. Take plenty of safety precautions (working from scaffolding rather than ladders, for example), and arrange for two or more experienced helpers.

FRAMING. Follow local codes to attach and flash the ledger board so it is very strong and protected from moisture. Install it 2 inches (5cm) or so below the threshold level.

Build the joist framing on temporary supports. On a raised deck like this, those temporary supports should be very strong. The supports will need to be heavily braced so that they do not move while you work. You may find it easier to first build the wide section, then the narrow section. Build rectangular joist framing sections; then mark and cut the two angled sections, and install angled header joists. Double the outside and header joists.

Build and temporarily attach beams under the joists. Use plumb lines to locate the positions of the postholes, and dig them according to code. Pour the footings. Make sure the joists are level; then measure for the length of the posts. Cut and install the posts, and backfill the postholes.

Install extra framing as needed so that the decking will be supported at all points. Near the house, install a row of blocking. Where the two decking angles will meet, supply framing for the border piece and the decking ends.

DECKING AND RAILING. Install railing posts before or after the decking, depending on the system you are using. Add blocking pieces as needed to make the posts firm.

Install the decking border along the house, as well as the border in the middle of the deck. Cut a series of decking pieces at 45 degrees where they will meet the border. Install the decking so that it runs past the framing. Mark the perimeters using a chalk line, and cut straight lines. Then install the other decking border pieces.

Attach the railing posts, and run electrical cable through them. Drill holes for the cables, and install the connections. Run the cables, and tighten. You will need to tighten them again later. Add the post caps and the top cap.

PERGOLA. This is a kit pergola that was ordered to fit the space; the manufacturer fashions the post and beam ends. Install the kit with the hardware provided. The canopy is also ordered to fit and installed according to the manufacturer's instructions.

MATERIALS

» FRAMING (ALL TREATED)
- ❑ 6x6 (15cmx15cm) posts
- ❑ 2x10s (5cmx25cm) for ledger and joists
- ❑ Double 2x10s (5cmx25cm) for beams
- ❑ Joist hangers

» FOOTINGS
- ❑ Concrete
- ❑ Tube forms
- ❑ Decking and Fascia 5/4x6 (3cmx15cm) composite decking, two colors
- ❑ Vinyl fascia

» RAILING
- ❑ Cable railing system, with composite posts

» PERGOLA
- ❑ 6x6 (15cmx15cm) hollow vinyl posts and beams, ordered to fit
- ❑ Canvas canopy and shade systems, ordered to fit

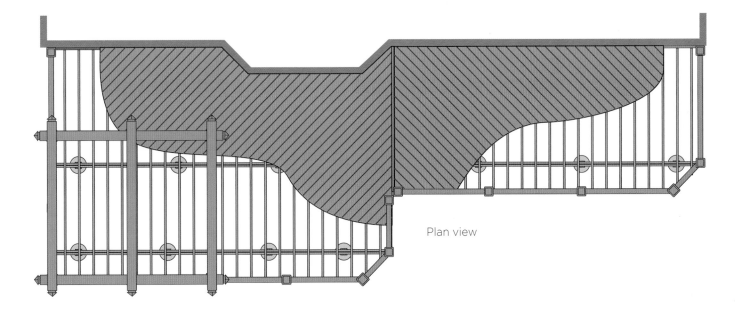

Plan view

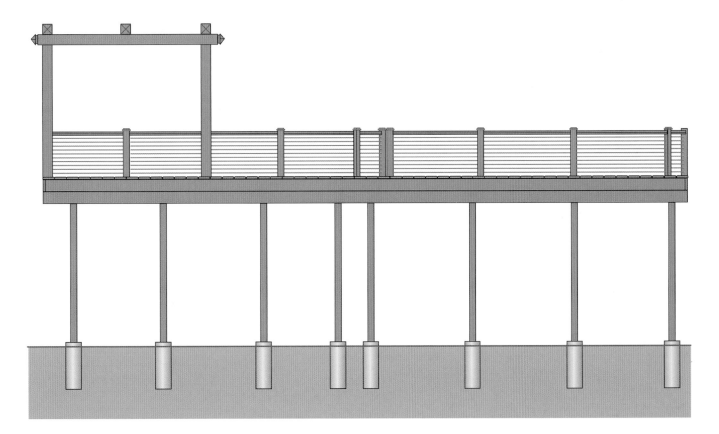

Elevation

Making It Dry under the Deck

If you have an upper-level deck, there are good reasons for keeping the area below dry. A dry patio or deck on the first floor can be a great place to enjoy your yard and to dine al fresco when the weather is wet. It can also be handy storage space. In addition, directing water away from the house can prevent damage to your basement walls.

The basic idea is to collect water that drips down between deck boards and direct it into a gutter. The gutter funnels water to a downspout, which carries water away from the house. Some systems fasten to the underside of the deck, while others use a membrane that attaches to the top of the joists.

Some dry-deck systems are better than others. Arana has developed his own, which uses an EPDM rubber membrane that is 1.1mm thick. Many companies use membranes that are only 0.25mm thick.

First, he measures and chalks lines for strips of rubber roofing that are wider at one end than the other, and cuts them using a knife or pair of shears. He then staples the strips to the tops of joists, with the wider part at the point where water will flow into the gutter. This makes the bottoms slope toward the gutter. At the other end of the joists, he staples short pieces that direct water in the other direction, again toward where the gutter will be.

The EPDM rubber roofing material reliably seals itself when fasteners are driven through it. For extra insurance against water infiltration, Arana staples narrow strips on top of the joists. At the house, he adds a flashing piece that slips up under the siding, to keep water away from the house. The decking is installed on top, and a gutter is installed below.

The dry area below this deck is used for a luxurious outdoor kitchen, with decorative lighting much like that used indoors.

Even if the patio under a deck will be a casual space, it's a good idea to keep it dry.

1 **Measure out the membrane.** Using 1.1mm-thick EPDM rubber membrane, measure and mark it for strips of rubber roofing that are wider at one end than the other by several inches.

2 **Cut the membrane.** Using shears, heavy-duty scissors, or a sharp utility knife, cut the strips of membrane as shown. Follow the cutting lines carefully.

3 **Install the long side.** You will likely place the gutter about 24 inches (61cm) from the outside of the deck. Install the long pieces of membrane, narrow to wide, from the house to this point.

4 **Install the short side.** Attach the shorter pieces of membrane to the deck's joists so that they direct water from the outside of the deck to the gutter.

5 **Attach sealing strips.** Although the rubber roofing membrane is self-sealing, it is a good idea to add a strip to the tops of the joists for extra sealing when you install the decking.

6 **Install flashing.** Insert a wide strip of the rubber membrane under the siding of the house so that it overlaps the decking membrane to form an effective water barrier.

Beautiful Symmetry

This project can be thought of as equal parts architectural feature and functioning deck. It completes the look of the house while also providing three wide-open spaces for almost any activity.

The Design

This deck's T-shape is the perfect complement to the house's partial U-shape. The house and deck work together as if they were built at the same time.

Symmetry is the rule, with some accommodations for the uniqueness of the site. The symmetrical elements: the home's stone fireplace is flanked by a sliding door on each side, and the central deck section is exactly as wide as these three elements. The front benches on each side are exact mirror images of each other. The decking pattern—45-degrees on each side and parallel with the house in the middle—neatly and obviously divides this spacious deck into three generous-sized rooms.

Accommodations for the site: on the left side, where the grill is placed, the yard slopes downward, making the deck higher than 30 inches (76cm) —which by code necessitates a railing. A railing could have been installed on the other side for the sake of looks, but it was felt that symmetry had been sufficiently employed.

Cable railing and low benches preserve the view from inside the house. The built-in benches are three decking boards—about 17 inches (43.2cm)—wide.

The decking is framed with decking boards of the same color for a subtle effect. Full-size border pieces are used in the middle. On each side of the center section, the front of the deck is framed with half-wide border pieces, made by rip-cutting decking. The decking overhangs the white fascia boards by just a ½ inch (1.3cm). Dividing the decking up in this way means that no butt joints are needed because no pieces are longer than 20 feet (6.1m).

Custom-made lattice skirting in a contrasting wood tone adds another level of appeal to the overall design. At the bottom of the front steps is a patio walkway made of large flagstones.

Setting flagstones. Large flagstones like these at the bottom of the steps must be carefully set in a gravel-and-sand base to keep them from cracking.

Fascia details. The fascia board was painted to match the off-white color of the railing. The ten decorative caps on the railing post can be removed to periodically tighten the cable.

Skirting. Stained cedar lattice skirting attractively makes the transition from the deck to the leafy landscape.

Decking border. On some parts of the perimeter a one-half-wide decking strip is used as a border.

Out-of-the-way grilling. Positioning a modest-size grill to the side minimizes discomfort from smoke.

Attention to detail. Perfect joints make all the difference in the feeling of a deck. Here, where exposed screw heads are needed, they are neatly arranged.

MATERIALS

» FRAMING (ALL TREATED)
- ❑ 6x6 (15cmx15cm) posts
- ❑ 2x8s (5cmx20cm) for ledger and joists
- ❑ Double 2x8s (5cmx20cm) for beams
- ❑ Joist hangers

» FOOTINGS
- ❑ Concrete
- ❑ Decking and Fascia 5/4x6 (3cmx15cm) composite decking,
- ❑ Vinyl fascia
- ❑ Cedar lattice

» RAILING
- ❑ Cable railing system, with composite posts

» BENCHES
- ❑ Treated 4x6 (10cmx15cm) posts
- ❑ Treated 2x4 (5cmx10cm) framing pieces
- ❑ Decking boards

Building the Deck

A low deck like this can be straightforward. Use treated lumber rated for ground contact where beams will come near the ground.

FRAMING AND CONCRETE. Attach and flash the ledger board 2 inches (5cm) or so below the threshold. On a low deck like this, it can be difficult to dig postholes after framing, so you may want to measure out from the ledger and dig the holes before framing. Make sure the postholes are in straight lines. Pour the concrete according to local code requirements.

Build the framing on temporary supports, which, in the case of a low deck, will not be difficult. Provide nailing surfaces for the borders and the decking ends; this means two joists about 6 inches (15.2cm) apart with blocking on each side of the middle section.

Build and attach the beams above the postholes. Cut and install the posts to support the beams, and backfill the holes. Install railing posts if they will be inside the framing.

DECKING AND BENCHES. Install the decking at a 45-degree angle on each side and parallel with the house in the middle. Where the different-angled decking boards meet, cut them to butt together tightly; they should be no farther than a decking board's width apart at any point. At the perimeters, allow the decking boards to run past the framing. Snap chalk lines, and carefully cut the decking; then set in the border pieces. On the perimeter, the boards should overhang by the thickness of the fascia, plus ½ inch (1.3cm) or so.

Install the cable railing according to manufacturer's instructions. Tighten the cables now, and do it again in a few days.

Frame for the long steps using box framing, as shown on page 82.

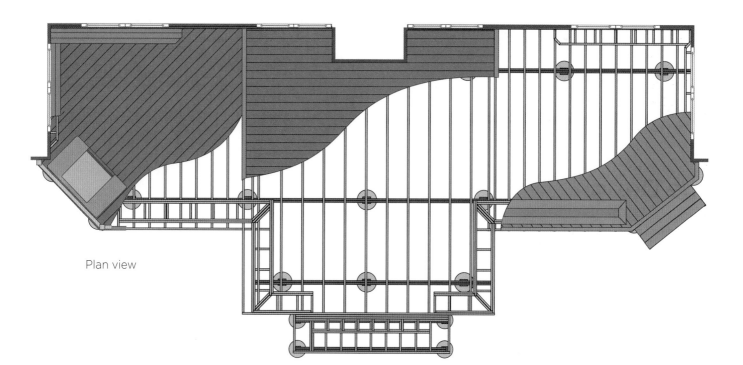

Plan view

Woodsy Retreat

Whimsically decorated for Halloween, this composite deck offers a range of creature comforts that accentuate the lovely woodsy setting.

The Design

The site had a patio held in place with a retaining wall, abutting a small rustic wood deck. The customers wanted something more finished-looking and larger. They do their grilling and serious dining elsewhere on the patio, so this space emphasizes an intimate gathering spot around a fire pit/table, and—most important—a sheltered spa.

DECK AND RAILING. The deck is a simple rectangle that extends out into a sloping yard, so its far end is about 8 feet (2.5m) above the ground. It is 20 feet (6.1m) wide and 24 feet (7.3m) long, plenty of space for a hot tub with

a hammock at the end and a small "sitting room" in the front. A modest grill could be placed to the right of the sitting room.

The decking is composite with a wood-grain look, simply run crosswise to take full advantage of the boards' 20-foot (6.1m) lengths. Where the deck meets the patio, one of the older decking boards is left in place for practical reasons: to remove it would have compromised the retaining wall that holds the paver patio in place. Leaving it there actually creates a nice transition between masonry and deck.

Spa area.
The spa is a plastic unit with faux brickwork. A set of two steps is needed for entering and exiting.

Accent balusters. Black railing balusters and rails make a classy contrast with the composite decking below and the ipé cap above.

Fireside comfort. A gas-fueled fire pit can be supplied via a gas line to the house or a propane tank below. The flames are adjustable and can be used for cooking hot dogs or marshmallows.

Soft lighting. The warm glow from soft lighting and a small fire make this leafy spa setting all the more inviting.

The railing is black composite with closely spaced round balusters. The black coordinates with the furniture and the light posts. It is capped with 5/4x6 (3cmx15cm) ipé decking. The lights you see on top of the railing are candles.

SPA AND OVERHEAD. Extra framing was required to support the spa, which rests on top of the decking. The position of the spa, at the end of the deck and with a pavilion roof overhead, makes the surrounding foliage feel like natural walls. Bathers can gaze at the trees, or turn around and converse with people sitting at chairs.

The overhead is not a pergola but an actual roof. The framing is made of large cedar timbers, with decorative bracing and a sunburst-like design at the gable end. It is an Amish design and was actually built by Amish workers. (See the sidebar on pages 102–103.) The metal roof makes a nostalgic plunking sound during rainfalls.

Building the Deck

This is a straightforward project in a basically rectangular shape. If, as on this job, one end is high in the air, follow safety precautions and work with helpers.

FRAMING. Here, a ledger board could be fastened to the retaining wall to help with the framing, but it was not considered structurally sound, so a beam with footings was installed 2 feet (61cm) away.

Install the framing on temporary supports, one decking board's thickness below the adjacent patio. Pour the concrete according to codes. Dig holes for three straight rows of footings. Add an extra row of footings to support a beam for the underside of the spa. Build and attach the beams under the joists. Measure, cut, and install 6x6 (15cmx15cm) posts that rest on the concrete and support the beams. Backfill the holes as required.

DECKING AND RAILING. Install railing posts inside the framing. Add pieces of blocking, and drive plenty of screws so that they will be firm.

The decking is simple. Install it to overhang the framing a bit; then snap chalk lines, and cut the decking flush with the outside of the framing. Install fascia board with its top edge flush with the deck surface.

Slip the railing post's sleeves over the posts, and cut the treated posts to height. Cut baluster sections to fit between the posts, and attach them using the brackets provided.

For installing the overhead, see pages 102–103.

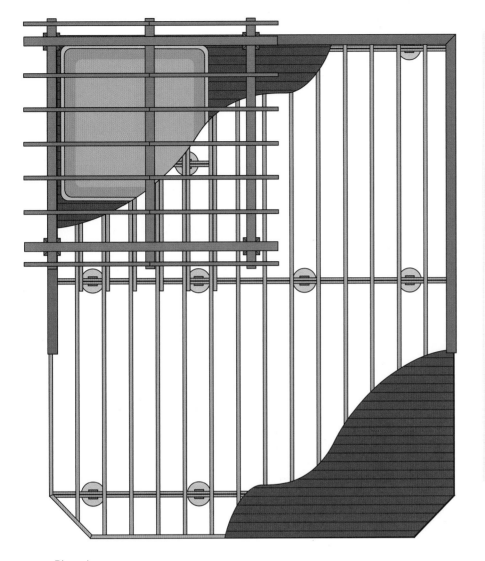

Plan view

MATERIALS

» **FRAMING (ALL TREATED)**
- ❏ 6x6 (15cmx15cm) posts
- ❏ 2x8s (5cmx20cm) for ledger and joists
- ❏ Double 2x8s (5cmx20cm) for beams
- ❏ Joist hangers

» **FOOTINGS**
- ❏ Concrete

» **DECKING AND FASCIA**
- ❏ 5/4x6 (3cmx15cm) composite decking
- ❏ Vinyl fascia

» **RAILING**
- ❏ 4x4 (10cmx10cm) treated posts
- ❏ Composite railing system
- ❏ 5/4x6 (3cmx15cm) ipé rail cap

» **OVERHEAD**
- ❏ A kit with cedar posts, beams, rafters, and braces
- ❏ Plywood roof sheathing
- ❏ Roofing felt (tar paper)
- ❏ Metal roofing

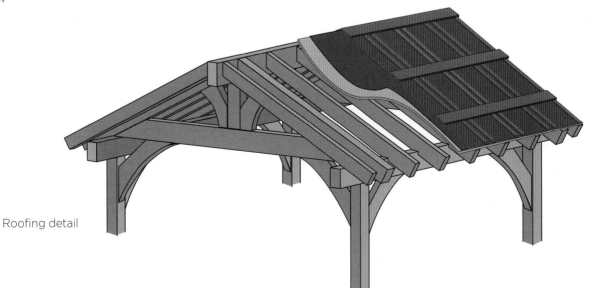

Roofing detail

An Amish Pavilion

The pavilion was purchased from the Amish company Penn Dutch Structures. (See the Resource Guide on page 216.) The company delivers kits all over the country, but these customers lived close enough to hire a crew to come and build it. Construction of this pavilion is, of course, nowhere near the complexity of the famous Amish barn raisings, but the easy cooperation of these young men is a thing of beauty. It took them only a few hours to build the frame. Once it was finished, roofers were hired to install plywood sheathing, roofing felt, and metal roofing.

This structure is made of cedar, but oak, pine, and other woods are also available. Large-dimension lumber like the 6x6s (15cmx15cm) and 6x8s (15cmx20cm) used here must be of very high quality, or they will almost certainly develop wide cracks.

The pavilion was built and assembled to make sure everything would fit, then disassembled and shipped to the site. Sections are reassembled, and metal anchors are attached to the bottoms of the posts.

Once the workers installed the side sections, they assembled and raised the gables into position to rest on top of the beams. They attached a 1x4 (2.5cmx10cm) board to the top of the gables using screws to help hold the structure temporarily during construction.

The workers drilled holes through the decking and installed a flat-laid piece of blocking under the decking for extra support. As they raised the side sections into position, they inserted anchors into the holes. From below the deck, they drove bolts up into the anchors.

The arched supports join together using splines, which are strips of wood inserted into grooves. The splines will not be visible.

The workers make all of the visible joinery using wooden pegs or dowels. Once they line up the holes in the pieces, they pound hardwood dowels through to make a firm connection. No glue or screws are required.

For more strength, the workers bore holes through the splines and drive more dowels.

Rafters fit neatly into V-slots that the workers routed in the ridge beam. They drove long screws through the top of the rafters into the ridge beam and into the beam at the other end; these screws will not be visible.

Lastly, the workers covered the roof with brown metal roofing that blends visually with its surroundings.

Woody Gem

Though comparatively small, long hardwood decking boards make this deck feel spacious, and the many angles and details in the design spice things up. Two clearly defined levels seem almost like two different decks.

The Design

Built around a favorite tree, this deck's dual levels define two separate use areas and make the overall semi-rectangular design much more interesting. Fine detail work in the construction adds depth to the design and makes the deck a pleasure to use.

SHAPE AND SIZE. The overall deck is approximately 12 x 30 feet (3.7m x 9.1m). The design features two odd angles: the front of the lower level near the tree is not quite parallel with the house, and at the step down from the upper to the lower level, the angle is a bit steeper, but still not the often-encountered 45 degrees. These unexpected angles make the deck feel as if it fits more naturally in its setting. The curved front of the upper level adds to the organic appeal.

The lower level comes as close as possible to a favorite tree without threatening its girth for another few decades. The resulting usable width is between 10 and 12 feet (3m and 3.7m), which is just enough room for a lounging or cooking area, or both. The upper level is clearly defined as an eating area, with room to maneuver all around the table.

MATERIALS. The beauty of ipé ironwood decking is on display here. Some of the decking boards on the lower level span a luxurious length exceeding 18 feet (5.5m). Because it needs no railing, the lower level makes a gracious transition to the yard.

The fascia for much of the deck is also ipé, but on the upper level's curved prow, white trim, one of Arana's signature finishing touches, gives the deck a finished appearance from the vantage point of the yard. The distinctive railing is also ipé, with side-mounted metal balusters reminiscent of old-fashioned cast iron railings that stylishly curve outward.

Dining area. The six-person rectangular table fits perfectly in the bumped-out space on the upper tier, a pleasant café distance from a smaller table on the tier below. A tall potted fern provides ambiance and privacy for the smaller table.

Craftsman carpentry. Joinery and craftsmanship make all the difference. Here, screw heads are sunk, filled, and sanded, producing rows of wood dots that look like dowels.

Unique railing details. Curved metal balusters attach to the sides of the top and bottom rails. The 1x4s (2.5cmx10cm) at the back of the posts cover a channel that was cut to run wiring for the post light.

Hidden detail. Arana pays attention to every little detail: even these tiny corners feature mitered joints and sunk-and-plugged fasteners.

Lighting fixtures. Black metal and stained ipé are a classic combination. The sconce helps light up the deck at night.

Building the Deck

This is a fairly straightforward deck to frame, but working with ipé is difficult and calls for quality tools and high-level skills in order to achieve tight joints.

FRAMING. Prepare the siding. and attach the ledger board with flashing so it will be firmly in place and protect the area from rainwater. Install one ledger for the upper level and another for the lower level. Build the frame for the lower level on temporary supports.

Build the upper level frame two steps up from the lower level. At the curved bump-out, allow the joists to run past where they need to go. Tack a board on top to keep them in position; then use a string-and-pencil compass to mark the tops of the joists for cutting on a curve. Cut each joist; you will need to adjust the bevel on your saw for each cut. Make the curved outside header by cutting ¾ inch (2cm)-deep kerfs in its back every 2 inches (5cm) or so; this will allow it to be bent. Attach the outside header. Then double all of the outside joists—including the curved header.

DECKING AND STEPS. Starting in the middle of each level, measure and install a decking board at 45 degrees to the house. Lay the rest of the decking, checking every few boards for straightness. To fasten the boards, drill a hole with a countersink bit; drive the screw; then squirt in some polyurethane glue and tap in a dowel. Sand the surface smooth after the glue has dried.

Build the steps with box framing, as shown on page 82.

RAILING AND FASCIA. Cut grooves and drill holes in the posts as needed to run the wiring for post lights. Notch the decking, and attach the posts to the outside of the header joists using two long lag bolts. Attach top and bottom rails to the inside faces of the railing posts. At the curved section, the rails must be cut at slight bevels for a tight fit. Cover the grooves and wiring with 1x4s (2.5cmx10cm) attached to the backs of the railing posts. Cap the railing off with decking pieces. Screw evenly spaced balusters to the top and bottom rails. Wire and install the post lights..

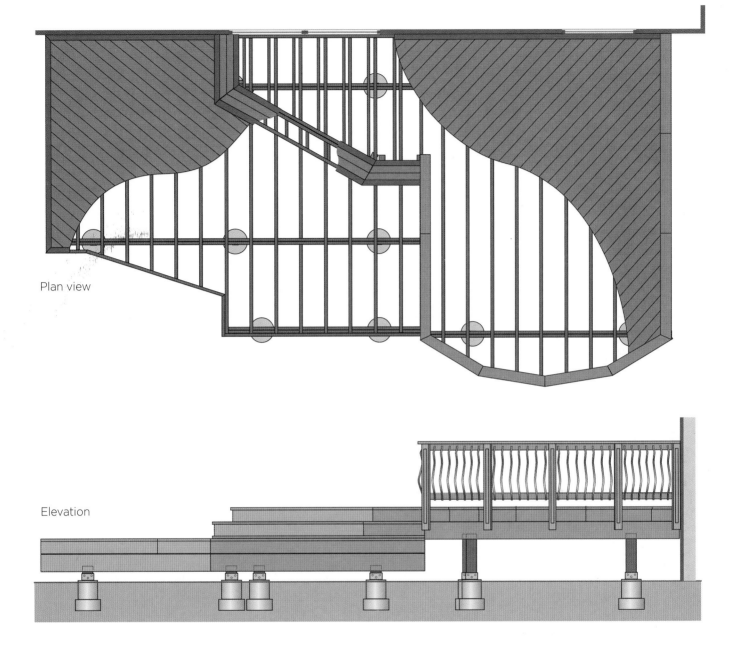

Plan view

Elevation

MATERIALS

» FRAMING (ALL TREATED)
- ❑ 6x6 (15cmx15cm) posts
- ❑ 2x8s (5cmx20cm) for ledger and joists
- ❑ Double 2x8s (5cmx20cm) for beams
- ❑ Joist hangers

» FOOTINGS
- ❑ Concrete

» DECKING AND FASCIA
- ❑ 5/4x6 (3cmx15cm) ipé decking
- ❑ Vinyl fascia

» RAILING
- ❑ 4x4 (10cmx10cm) ipé posts
- ❑ 2x4 (5cmx10cm) ipé top and bottom rails
- ❑ 5/4x6 (3cmx15cm) ipé top cap
- ❑ Metal side-mounted balusters

Barrett Outdoors

Gus de la Cruz operates Barrett Construction in New Jersey, a fairly large business that keeps three or four crews busy much of the time. He builds about 50 decks a year. The company has won numerous building and designing awards.

He does much of his work in the rural central part of the state, which is surprisingly pretty and woodsy, despite the impression many have of New Jersey based on popular culture and reality shows. Stately homes share the landscape with farmland, and decks tend to be large. He also builds decks in more populated areas near the shore—in these areas, decks tend to be smaller.

The Barrett company—named after Syd Barrett of Pink Floyd, a favorite of de la Cruz's—is a full-service backyard company. In addition to building decks, de la Cruz constructs patios, outdoor kitchens, and roofs for porches, and even deals in outdoor furniture. By the time this book is published, he will have a showroom where customers can view a variety of products and surfaces.

Surprising shapes. A flamboyantly scalloped shape is oriented toward a lovely woodsy view and is just the right size for a sheltered dining area. The clean lines and simple colors of composite decking and PVC railings make a design statement by themselves, yet are neutral enough to work as a background for any color scheme.

Gustavo "Gus" de la Cruz

BARRETT OUTDOORS

Millstone Township, New Jersey
866-418-1891
www.barrettoutdoors.com

Metal framing. Metal joists make for a perfectly flat deck surface, and an under-deck drainage system funnels water to a nearby gutter, keeping the area beneath dry.

Natural touches. Large potted plants soften the transition between house and deck and add their special garden charm.

DESIGNING AROUND THE FURNITURE

Gus describes his design approach as pragmatic, first of all addressing the needs and wants of the homeowners. He says the first question should not be "How big?" but "How will you use the deck?" He listens closely, then uses computer design programs to develop plans that help the customer envision the finished product. He has several programs from which to choose, depending on the complexity of the job.

It often works best to start with what many people buy at the end—the furniture. For instance, a large family that often entertains may need a dining table for eight, but a smaller urban family may prefer a four-seater. Families with children may want play areas for a swing set or a small pool; those inclined to lounge with a book at the end of the day will probably want a pair of comfortable chairs with a small table. Once the furniture pieces have been selected, the deck can be designed so that traffic will flow easily around use areas, with special attention to clear paths from the kitchen to the grill and the dining areas and out to the stairs that lead to the yard.

DESIGNS THAT POP

Whether they are looking for a massive big-budget deck or a more modest one, de la Cruz's customers usually want a deck that is distinctive. They usually know from the start that they want a certain feature, such as a gentle curve, an odd angle, a half-circle, an octagon, or stairs at 45 degrees to the deck. A good deck design does not need to have a lot of design splashes, but it should have one or two. An unusual element or two makes a deck unique.

While angles certainly add interest, curves make a deck feel more organic. Gus takes special pride in his curved areas and has purchased expensive equipment to ensure that he gets the best results.

Decks and patios. Gus's outdoor projects often combine a deck with a patio, aiming for separate outdoor rooms that work well together.

Unique countertops. This outdoor kitchen features two spacious, curved granite counters, one for cooking, and one for dining.

Defined spaces. This large second-floor deck has room for two generously proportioned dining areas, as well as an outdoor kitchen and several lounging areas.

Natural light. As the sun goes down and shadows lengthen, a dreamy ambiance descends to make this deck a lovely place for dining or relaxing.

Kitchen convenience. This outdoor kitchen features a stainless-steel refrigerator and grill, composite cabinets, and touches of faux-stone facing.

Expert joinery. Ipé decking is cut and joined with craftsman's care and attention to detail.

Excellent craftsmanship. New materials—composite decking, PVC rail posts, and metal balusters—are lovingly cut with perfect joinery that will retain its integrity for many decades.

OUTDOOR KITCHENS AND LIGHTING

Only a minority of de la Cruz's decks have outdoor kitchens, but they are growing in popularity. He builds with fairly lightweight materials that can rest on a well-built deck. Many of his kitchens have just the basics—a grill with countertop plus storage space below. But some include side burners, sinks, and other amenities.

Most of his decks incorporate lighting, and de la Cruz prides himself on careful placement so that a deck will be evenly lit and safe to walk on. Lighting should be adequate for seeing where you are but should be moderate and soft rather than glaring. Nearly all of his lights are energy-saving LEDs. A combination of lights on post caps, the sides of posts, and stair risers, as well as in the landscape, can produce a stunning effect when the sun goes down.

DECKING AND RAILING MATERIALS

Though he is certainly not averse to building wood decks, de la Cruz finds that most people in New Jersey prefer low-maintenance composite and PVC materials. Many have grown tired of the regular cleaning and staining required for wood decks and are relieved to have surfaces that need only a quick sweep or hosing off. He installs decking with no visible screw or nail heads.

de la Cruz's Techniques

1 More and more of de la Cruz's decks are built using metal framing. He uses metal joists and beams, manufactured by a decking company, which are galvanized and powder-coated. Metal framing is stronger than same-size wood framing, which means it can run for longer spans—requiring fewer posts—with the result that there is more usable space below the deck. Because metal joists are perfectly straight, they make for wonderfully flat deck surfaces. (Wood joists typically are at least slightly crowned, and composite decking shows these imperfections more clearly than wood decking.) Metal decking is approved in most areas of the country, but not in wet climates; for instance, it is not allowed within 3,000 feet (914.4m) of a body of water.

2 Gus designs to avoid any butt joints in the decking, which means that no decking run can be longer than 20 feet (6.1m). To accomplish this and to add design detail, he often frames decking sections with divider strips (or "breaker boards") running across the middle of the deck surface. He also often frames the deck's perimeter with decking boards that frame the deck for a more finished look.

3 He often runs decking in two or more directions. This not only makes the deck more interesting to look at, but also helps define use areas and reduce tripping hazards. The overall look is more distinctive when use areas are on different levels.

4 He usually uses composite decking boards that have grooves on the side edges to accept hidden fasteners, so no fastener heads are visible. This material is more expensive but results in a deck surface that is neater in appearance and easier to clean because dirt cannot collect at the fasteners. When installing ipé or other wood, he uses different hidden fastener hardware.

5 Gus builds extra strong. Where most codes require a deck to be strong enough to support a 40-pound "live load," his decks are engineered for 60 pounds or more. The result is a deck that feels solid and without any bounce.

6 When installing in-ground posts, he uses 6x6s (15cmx15cm) rated for "permanent foundation" use, which are more resistant to rot than boards rated for "ground contact." Permanent-foundation boards may have to be special-ordered and cost a bit more, but they ensure that the deck's structure will not rot.

7 Gus often uses plastic footing "feet" rather than pouring concrete footings. These units install quickly, saving money, and have been engineered to provide more-than-adequate support.

8 For upper-level decks with living space below, he offers an under-deck drainage system that funnels rainwater dripping between deck boards to a gutter and downspout, keeping the lower patio or deck dry. The system is similar to Arana's (pages 92–93), but de la Cruz prefers to place the gutter outside the deck.

Jewel by the Pool

This medium-size deck adds plenty of outdoor living space: a generous dining area, an outdoor kitchen, and a sheltered living room. With natural ipé wood decking, stone pillars, and an artfully rounded front, it is also stunning to look at.

The Design

The first idea was to provide a deck surface with a clear view of the swimming pool and patio so that adults could easily monitor kids below while relaxing and eating. Another priority was a large dining area and grilling station to accommodate family meals and medium-size gatherings of friends.

The main (lower) deck addresses those needs. A table large enough for six or eight fits comfortably near the outdoor kitchen and takes up about half the space, leaving plenty of room for potted plants or conversation areas.

Children often revel in weather's variations while adults tend to prefer shelter from sun or rain. The upper deck is covered by a roof while maintaining an open orientation to the rest of the deck and yard. A couch with small table against the wall is a great place to toast the day's successes in comfort. When the weather gets oppressive, there is room to add more chairs.

CURVINESS. The signature 10-foot-radius (3m) curve in this ironwood deck greatly increased the difficulty and expense of the project, but everyone agreed it just felt right. The stairs leading to the patio are also curved, with the same radius as the deck, adding stylish symmetry.

ROOF WITH PILLARS. Gus built the roof at the same time as the deck. It is a real roof with shingles, not just an overhead structure, so it needs solid support. To hold up the roof stylishly, he constructed two pairs of pillars with a 15-foot (4.6m) space between, which preserves the open layout while still clearly marking out the different rooms.

Structurally, the pillars are made using posts that rest on the deck's main beam. Pressure-treated 6x6 (15cmx15cm) posts rise to about 4 feet (1.2m) above the deck; they are boxed in with plywood, which is covered with faux stones (nearly indistinguishable from the real thing). Classic-looking white pillars of composite material run from the top of the post-and-stone structures to the underside of the roof. The pillar/stone combination has a casual elegance that elevates the overall deck design.

Unique rails. Curved top and bottom rails are made with ipé that is stained darker than the rest of the deck.

Outdoor kitchen. The outdoor kitchen, or grilling station, nestles unobtrusively against the stone pillars. The decking's picture-frame piece runs around it.

Access door. A simple door with hinges reminiscent of a barn door provides access to space beneath the deck, used for storage and utilities.

Curved stairs. The stairs are curved, but bending ipé decking into a curve like this is impossible, so they are curve-cut on their edges. Nice wide stairs are always an inviting hangout spot.

Framing pieces. The outer edge of the curved part of the deck is framed using 1½-inch-wide (4cm) pieces that run between the railing posts.

Expert craftsmanship. Details make all the difference in a fine deck, and de la Cruz's are exquisite.

OUTDOOR KITCHEN. The grilling station, or outdoor kitchen, nestled against the side of the deck and two of the stone pillars, blends naturally with the rest of the setting. The faux stone siding matches the base of the pillars, and the soft, neutral-colored granite is the perfect complement. This is a fairly modest outdoor kitchen, with a large gas grill, one set of access doors for storage below, and about 6 running feet (1.8m) of countertop space. That is enough for most grilling preparation work, plus an area for mixing a salad; if you want to do additional cooking or work with a helper or two, you may want a larger counter.

Upper deck.
The view from the upper deck is all the more bright and pleasing when contemplated from the vantage point of shady comfort.

DECKING AND RAILING. The decking is ipé, a Brazilian ironwood that will last a very long time. Unlike composite decking, it needs to be cleaned and re-stained on a yearly basis. The owners feel that is a small price to pay for the natural beauty.

The decking runs parallel with the house. A central divider strip bisects both upper and lower deck neatly in half, and "picture frame" decking pieces around the perimeter are satisfying finishing touches.

The deck's railing posts, as well as the top and bottom rails, are also ipé. Making the curves with hardwood is time-consuming and expensive but more in keeping with the curved prow of the deck than straight sections would have been. The balusters (pickets) are round aluminum. Because they are narrow, they barely inhibit the view. The stair railing is all metal.

Building the Deck

Use high-quality No. 1 or No. 2 pressure-treated lumber for the framing. For posts that will be sunk in the ground, use treated lumber rated for "permanent foundation."

FRAMING. Lay out and dig holes for the row of footings that will support the beam near the house. Pour concrete footings as required by code. Set the posts in the holes. Attach the ledger with code-approved flashing at the house, and measure off it to mark the posts for cutting. See the illustration "elevation detail" on page 121 to help determine the height.

Build the middle beam by laminating three 2x8s (5cmx20cm). Use hardware to fasten the beam on top of the posts. Mark the top of the beam with the positions of the four roof-support posts. Build the joist framing for the lower deck, setting joists on the beam at one end and on temporary supports at the other. Install double joists at the sides. Install special framing for the decking's divider board, as shown on page 121. As you build, make sure the joists do not get in the way of the roof-support posts; you may need to change their spacing to accommodate the posts. Install the lower-deck joists running wild, i. e., longer than they need to be. Dig holes, and install posts and beams to support the joists.

Install blocking near the end of joist runs where the curve will be. To mark the tops of the joists for the curve, use a mason's line as a long compass: locate the point that is at the exact center of the circle—halfway between the deck sides and an equal distance from the front of the curve. (It will probably be between two joists, so you will need to attach a piece of plywood.) Partially drive a screw into this point. Fasten one end of the string to the screw. Measure out the desired radius of the curve, and tie a pencil to the other end. Holding the string taut, mark the tops of the joists for cutting the curve.

Use a square to mark for end cuts at each of the lines you just drew. For each cut, you will need to change the bevel on your circular saw. (These bevels do not have to be precise, but they should be pretty close.) To make the header, rip-cut pieces of ½ inch (1.3cm) treated plywood to the width of the joists, and screw them in three layers to the cut joist ends. Overlap the joints, so that two joints do not occur at the same joist.

At the end of the lower deck framing nearest the house, build a knee wall with 2x6 (5cmx15cm) top and bottom plates and 2x6 (5cmx15cm) studs every 16 inches (40.6cm) to support the upper-level framing at the same height as the ledger. Construct the joist framing for the

upper level, again making sure that you do not interfere with the 6x6 (15cmx15cm) roof-support posts.

DECKING. Install the divider boards that run down the middle of the two deck levels. Starting with a full decking board against the house, install the decking on both levels, allowing it to run long at each end. Use hidden fasteners. Where the deck's perimeter is straight, snap a chalk line, and cut the decking boards flush with the outside of the framing.

To cut the decking curves, use a router with a cutoff bit. Make a compass using a long board, attaching it to the center of the circle at one end with a nail and to the router at the other end. Cut the decking along the outside of the plywood header.

RAILING, FASCIA, AND DECKING TRIM. Install the railing posts against the outside framing, drilling holes and attaching lag bolts or carriage bolts to firmly fasten it. (In some locales you are required to install special railing post hardware.)

Where the deck's perimeter is straight, install 2x4 (5cmx10cm) blocking pieces, then the fascia board between the posts to provide support for the picture-frame decking piece. Cut picture-frame pieces the same width as the posts to fit between the posts, and attach them using screws.

Where the deck's perimeter curves, attach the fascia without 2x4 (5cmx10cm) blocking. Use your long compass to mark decking pieces for curve cuts, and cut curved pieces that are 1½ inches (4cm) wide. Cut them to fit between the rail posts, and attach them by driving screws into the fascia board.

Use the long compass to cut 1-by (2.5cm-by) ipé pieces for the top and bottom rails. Make each rail by laminating two 1-by (2.5cm-by) layers together using polyurethane glue. Attach the rails and the balusters between the posts.

STAIRS. Build a large number of stair stringers for the steps between the two levels, and attach them to the lower-level decking and to the fascia between the two levels. Also build stringers for the steps leading to the yard, and attach them to the fascia and to a masonry landing pad in the yard. Make the treads out of decking boards, and cover the risers with fascia board. Have a fabricator make metal railings to fit the steps leading to the yard.

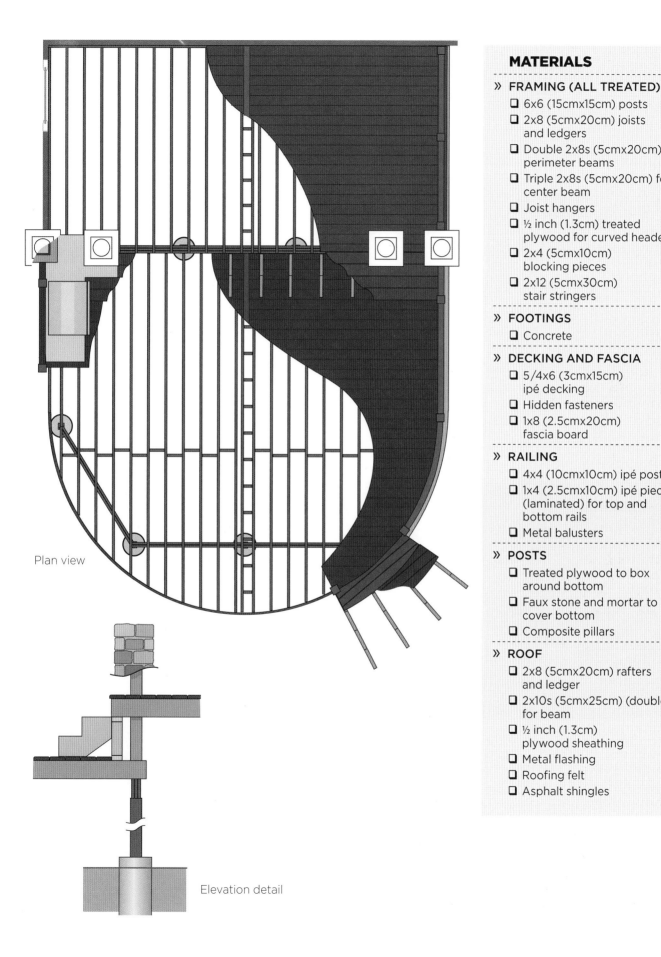

Plan view

Elevation detail

MATERIALS

» **FRAMING (ALL TREATED)**
- ❏ 6x6 (15cmx15cm) posts
- ❏ 2x8 (5cmx20cm) joists and ledgers
- ❏ Double 2x8s (5cmx20cm) for perimeter beams
- ❏ Triple 2x8s (5cmx20cm) for center beam
- ❏ Joist hangers
- ❏ ½ inch (1.3cm) treated plywood for curved header
- ❏ 2x4 (5cmx10cm) blocking pieces
- ❏ 2x12 (5cmx30cm) stair stringers

» **FOOTINGS**
- ❏ Concrete

» **DECKING AND FASCIA**
- ❏ 5/4x6 (3cmx15cm) ipé decking
- ❏ Hidden fasteners
- ❏ 1x8 (2.5cmx20cm) fascia board

» **RAILING**
- ❏ 4x4 (10cmx10cm) ipé posts
- ❏ 1x4 (2.5cmx10cm) ipé pieces (laminated) for top and bottom rails
- ❏ Metal balusters

» **POSTS**
- ❏ Treated plywood to box around bottom
- ❏ Faux stone and mortar to cover bottom
- ❏ Composite pillars

» **ROOF**
- ❏ 2x8 (5cmx20cm) rafters and ledger
- ❏ 2x10s (5cmx25cm) (doubled) for beam
- ❏ ½ inch (1.3cm) plywood sheathing
- ❏ Metal flashing
- ❏ Roofing felt
- ❏ Asphalt shingles

Metal Framing

In recent years, de la Cruz and some other deck builders have been building decks with metal framing. Joists, ledgers, and beams are the most common metal structural members, but metal posts are also available.

Metal framing costs more than wood, adding perhaps as much as $4 per square foot (0.09m²) to the cost of a deck. However, it has distinct advantages.

Metal framing is almost perfectly straight and will not shrink, warp, or crack. That means that deck floors are almost perfectly flat and will stay that way.

It is stronger than wood framing of the same dimensions. That not only means a firmer deck; it can also mean you need fewer beams and posts—which can free up space below and lower overall construction costs. A wood 2x8 (5cmx20cm) joist, for instance, typically has an allowable span of 12 feet (3.7m), while a metal 2x8 (5cmx20cm) joist can span up to 15 feet (4.6m).

Some metal framing is stronger than others, depending on the thickness of the steel. Most types are galvanized and powder-coated to resist rusting. Many products are guaranteed not to rust for 25 years. However, local codes may bar their use close to large bodies of water or in a humid climate.

Framing for curves is much easier using metal because you can buy special flexible header pieces.

Much metal framing is gray, but other colors, including dark brown and black, are also available. The surface looks good enough that you may choose to let it show, and go without fascia board.

Both joists and beams look great.

Straight silver-gray metal joists have a neat appearance.

Metal posts have a finished look but may not be permitted for in-ground use.

A curved header is easy to form using metal framing.

Special hardware and other pieces make it easy to add features such as blocking.

Curvy Party Deck

The existing deck here was pretty dismal: it was not only poorly constructed and falling apart, but also a narrow and boring rectangle shape. The customers wanted a large space for entertaining, with a varied mix of spacious rooms for sit-down dining, relaxed conversation, barroom tippling, grilling, and sitting around a fire pit. They also wanted a deck with memorable style, which de la Cruz supplied using stylish curves, a roof with flying rafters, and a few other nice details.

The Design

A long site like this provides space for multiple "rooms." The trick is to make it flow easily while clearly defining different use areas. Two doors lead to the deck. The sliding door on the left (as you look at the deck from the yard) emerges from the house's living room, so it is natural to make this portion of the deck an extension of that living space, with a large semicircular sofa and a small table for snacks and reading matter. This living room is raised one step above the rest of the deck.

Walking one step down from the living room, you meet the stairway to the yard, which is positioned within easy reach from the living room or the dining area. The dining area has plenty of space for a large table, as well as wider-than-usual traffic paths—which are important when hosting large groups.

Moving on from the dining room, you encounter an outdoor kitchen with two counters; the eating counter with stools is perfect for socializing with the chef(s). The roof overhead makes it possible to cook even during rain. And moving on from there, you walk a step down to a patio with lounge furniture and a fire pit. All in all, there are at least four distinct rooms, with four different ways to meet and greet family and friends.

Unique angles. A 2½-foot-wide (76cm) landing by the utility door is wide enough for comfortably entering and exiting the house. Adding an angle creates just a touch of geometric interest.

Living room. A spacious outdoor living room, outfitted with comfortable furniture, is within easy communication of the interior living room.

Beautiful construction. The stairway and landing leading to the yard offer an opportunity to showcase de la Cruz's conscientious craftsmanship.

CURVES. The customers wanted something different style-wise, and de la Cruz suggested gentle curves. The curves have no practical purpose; they just make the design more fun and interesting. A curve this modest has a 16-foot (4.9m) radius, and the deck is 16 feet (4.9m) wide, so if you were to make a string-and-pencil compass and put one end of the compass up against the house, you would end up with this curve. By comparison, the deck shown on pages 116–121 has a 10-foot (3m) radius.

Unique curves. Sinuous curves define the unique look of the deck.

The two curves give the deck an organic, meandering quality, accented by the color contrast between dark decking and white railing and fascia. The overall design is bright and buoyant and perks up the view of the home's exterior.

OUTDOOR KITCHEN AND PATIO. Two facing 8-foot-long (2.5m) kitchen counters, about 4 feet (1.2m) apart, give the cook and perhaps a helper or two plenty of room to maneuver. One counter houses a large 4-foot (1.2m) gas grill with about 2 feet (61cm) of counter space on each side and utility doors for storage below. On the other side, a second grill has countertops at two levels: one level is a standard 36 inches (91cm) high and houses a sink, providing a great place to mix drinks and to prepare salads and veggies. The other level is 42 inches (1.1m) high and cantilevers out 12 inches (30.5cm), so people in bar stools can sip drinks or munch on hors d'oeuvres while conversing with each other and with the cook.

The outdoor kitchen is protected by a gable roof that ties into the house's roof. It is supported by classic-looking pillars, and its ceiling has recessed lights and a ceiling fan. From the kitchen, the deck leads down two steps to a paver patio. The patio is partially surrounded by a stone-topped wall and has a central medallion section, which houses a gas fire pit.

MATERIALS AND COLORS. Composite decking and railings will retain their pristine appearance and will be easy to maintain. The white railings, fascia, and trim add geometric clarity that plays off the house trim. Overall, the deck gives one the feeling of a house addition rather than a tacked-on deck.

Spacious dining area. Even with a large table for six, this dining room has a spacious, open feel that makes it inviting. Splashes of color from textiles brighten up the neutral palette of the space.

Curved frame. The perimeter picture-frame decking pieces are curved, and adjacent straight decking boards are carefully cut to match that curve.

Patio space. As if all that deck space weren't enough, a handsome patio adds even more space for outdoor enjoyment.

Overhead options. The overhead ceiling is covered with painted bead board and dotted with recessed canister lights. A ceiling fan helps keep things cool and blows away grilling smoke.

Countertop space. Two countertop levels add versatility to the kitchen, providing space for both mixologist and drinkers. A small bar sink is all that is usually needed in an outdoor kitchen. This side of the granite counter is faced with decking; the other side is faced with faux stone.

Building the Deck

Installing curved composite decking calls for special equipment. (See pages 130–131.) Build the deck frame with pressure-treated lumber and plywood; use posts rated for permanent foundation work. As an alternative, you can build with metal framing, as shown on pages 122–123. Choose decking with hidden fasteners and a PVC railing system.

FRAMING. Attach a ledger, with code-approved flashing, for each of the decking levels. Position the ledgers so that the decking will end up about 1½ inches (4cm) below the house's threshold. Install the lower ledger 7½ inches (19.1cm) below the upper ledger.

Build joist framing for the different levels by attaching them with joist hangers to the ledgers and on temporary supports at the other end. Install blocking, if required. Here, joists are 16 inches (40.6cm) apart, but place them 12 inches (30.5cm) apart or closer if the decking will run diagonally. For sections with curves, install the joists to run longer than they need to be.

Install blocking to make sure all joists are spaced apart the same distances as they are at the ledger. Make a long string-and-pencil compass to mark the tops of the joists at the curved sections. Mark each side of each joist for end cuts, and adjust the circular saw slightly for each cut.

To make the curved header, cut strips of pressure-treated plywood the same width as the joists. Attach the plywood to the ends of the joists. Cut the pieces so that joints occur at the middle of the joists. Install three layers of plywood, offsetting the joints from layer to layer.

Dig straight rows of postholes where the beams will go. Make the beams by doubling 2x8s (5cmx20cm) and attaching them to the underside of the joists, above the holes. Pour concrete into the holes as required by code, or use plastic post footings. Set the posts; cut them to height; and attach them to the underside of the beam.

In the spot where the stairway to the yard will go, frame around the opening. Cut stringers, and attach them to the framing at the top. At the bottom, frame a landing for the stringers to rest on; the frame should be supported by posts, or it can rest on a small concrete or masonry pad.

Run plumbing and electrical lines for the outdoor kitchen, deck lighting, and ceiling lights for the roof.

DECKING AND RAILING. Install the 4x4 (10cmx10cm) railing posts, attached to the inside of the framing with blocking as shown in the illustration on page 129.

Install curved decking pieces to follow the curves. To bend composite decking, see pages 130–131. Test the pieces for the correct curvature, but do not attach them yet. Lay the decking pieces that will be next to the curved pieces on the joists, and use a measuring tape and chalk line to see that they are straight and parallel with the house. Lay the curved pieces on top; they should overhang the framing by the thickness of the fascia, plus ¾ inch (2cm). Use the curved pieces as templates to mark for curved cuts. Make cuts using a circular saw or jigsaw. Install the curve-cut pieces, then the outside curved pieces. Then install the rest of the decking.

Install PVC post sleeves over the railing posts. Use the same forms as you used for the curved decking pieces to curve the railing pieces. Cut them to length so that they fit between the posts. Assemble the rails' balusters; then attach the sections (called balustrades) to the posts using the hardware provided.

Install PVC fascia under the decking. Attach treads on the stair stringers, and add fascia boards to the risers. For the small landing on the lower level, build a simple 2x8 (5cmx20cm) frame, and cover it with decking and fascia.

OUTDOOR KITCHEN AND ROOF. Build the outdoor kitchen out of wood or metal framing, sheathed with backer board and covered by faux stone or decking. Add countertops, a grill, and sink. (See Creative Homeowner's *Building Outdoor Kitchens for Every Budget* for full instructions.)

Build the roof by installing the posts, then the beams. Add rafters with a ridge beam, and tie it into the house in a code-approved way. Add ceiling joists. Cover the rafters with plywood; then add roofing felt, flashings, gutters, and shingles. Run wiring, and attach lights and a ceiling fan box to the ceiling joists. Cover the underside of the joists with bead board, and install the light trims and the ceiling fan. Add the decorative "flying" rafter pieces to the sides; they are not structural and simply attach to the fascia.

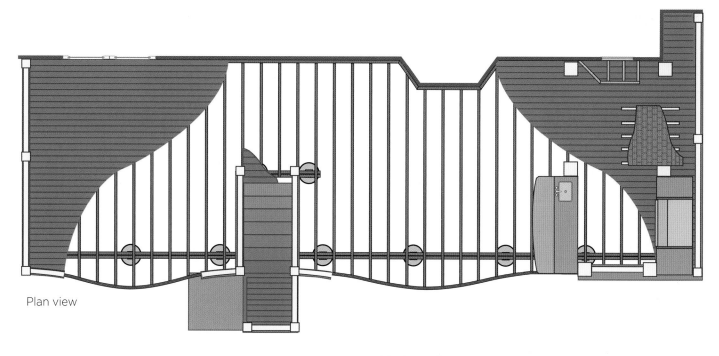

Plan view

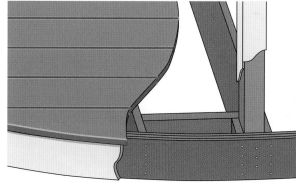

Post detail

MATERIALS

» **FRAMING (ALL TREATED)**
- ❏ 6x6 (15cmx15cm) posts
- ❏ 2x8 (5cmx20cm) joists and ledger
- ❏ Double 2x8s (5cmx20cm) for beams
- ❏ Joist hangers
- ❏ ½ inch (1.3cm) treated plywood for curved header
- ❏ 2x8 (5cmx20cm) blocking pieces
- ❏ 2x12 (5cmx30cm) stair stringers

» **FOOTINGS**
- ❏ Concrete

» **DECKING AND FASCIA**
- ❏ 5/4x6 (3cmx15cm) composite decking
- ❏ Hidden fasteners
- ❏ 1x8 (2.5cmx20cm) fascia board

» **RAILING**
- ❏ 4x4 (10cmx10cm) posts
- ❏ PVC sleeves for posts
- ❏ PVC top and bottom rails
- ❏ Metal balusters

» **ROOF**
- ❏ PVC pillars
- ❏ 2x8 (5cmx20cm) rafters and ledger
- ❏ 2x10s (5cmx25cm) (doubled) for beam
- ❏ ½ inch (1.3cm) plywood sheathing
- ❏ Metal flashing
- ❏ Roofing felt
- ❏ Asphalt shingles
- ❏ Bead board
- ❏ Recessed lights and a ceiling fan

Bending Composite Decking and Railing

Building framing for deck curves is challenging but doable for a person with good carpentry skills. (If you use metal framing, it is easier.) But bending highly visible decking or railing into smooth curves is a good deal more difficult and calls for special equipment that generally costs $5,000–$10,000. Here we'll show some methods for bending composite and vinyl pieces.

Decking or rails must be heated hot enough so that they can be bent but not so hot that the pieces actually start to melt. This can be done with a special oven (see below right) or a heating blanket (see top right on page 131).

Determining the right curve calls for careful measuring and marking. Make a jig that follows the correct curve. Once a piece is thoroughly heated, clamp it against the jig.

Here top and bottom rails, as well as a dark-colored picture-frame piece on the decking perimeter, are bent to the same curve profile.

A special decking oven, which can be wheeled to the construction site, can handle 8-foot-long (2.5m) boards. It usually takes about a half hour to heat each board.

130

Once bent, the boards must be tightly clamped in a form.

A blanket heater makes it possible to bend longer pieces. A board is placed between heating pads, which are covered with fiberglass insulation.

The readout on the controller tells when the board is ready for bending.

This clamping method uses a series of boards cut at the right curve. The boards on one side are attached to a sheet of plywood, and the boards on the other side are clamped.

131

Relaxation Station

This modest-sized deck satisfies the owners' unpretentious goal: to provide a gracious space for enjoying the peace and quiet of the backyard. Graceful angles bring the engaging shape to life.

Patio space. The adjacent patio, made of concrete pavers, is easy to keep clean. These pavers have a variety of hues for a subtle, natural charm. Eclectic furniture and a fire pit add to the casual appeal.

The Design

The owners were not interested in heavy-duty grilling or formal outdoor dining, and they already had a good-size paver patio for gatherings. They pretty much just wanted a place that felt like a comfortable seating area.

SHAPE AND SIZE. Sometimes a small, simple change can make all the difference. The existing, narrow rectangular deck lacked "flow" in two ways: moving around on it was often awkward because of a bottleneck when people sat on chairs; and it just felt boxy. Gus de la Cruz solved these problems by bumping it out an additional 5 feet (1.5m) away from the house at one end, and he did this with a 45-degree angle.

The change eliminated traffic flow problems and gave the deck a spacious, open feel with plenty of legroom for people in lounge chairs and plenty of space for potted plants. The bumped-out area is also just wide enough for a six-person dining table, should they choose to add one in the future.

In some ways this deck feels like a larger-than-average front porch. It has a narrow section that functions simply as a walkway to the driveway. But because it is 6 feet (1.8m) wide rather than the more common 4 feet (1.2m), it feels like a usable space; the grill comfortably resides here, or it can be wheeled out to the wider area when needed.

MATERIALS. The decking and the railing are similar in color, forming a soothing monochromatic palette agreeable with the landscape. Lighter tones in the lattice skirting, which is only about 2 feet (61cm) tall, perk up the view from the yard or patio.

All visible parts of the deck and rail are made of high-quality composite for easy maintenance. This is especially welcome in a woodsy setting; organic matter like seeds and leaves accumulate and would be a cleaning headache for other surfaces.

Wide layout. The main deck is 12 feet (3.7m) wide in one section, then opens to 18 feet (5.5m) wide. Potted plants scattered casually make the deck feel cozy.

Joinery details. Careful cutting and joinery make composite materials seem like natural wood.

Gravel border. The gravel border beneath the deck's skirting, attractively framed by Belgium blocks, absorbs runoff from the deck.

Casual seating. A modest arrangement of wood-and-fabric furniture, dotted with throw pillows, preserves the spacious appeal of this sun-dappled deck.

Building the Deck

On a deck this small, de la Cruz finds that it is easier to install posts and beams first (rather than building the joist framing on temporary supports and adding posts and beams later). For more information on metal framing, see pages 122-123.

FRAMING. Install the ledger 2½ inches (6.5cm) below the house's threshold, which will put the finished deck surface 1½ inches (4cm) below the threshold. A metal ledger is a channel rather than a solid piece. Metal joists attach to the ledger via special angle brackets.

Dig straight lines of postholes to support the beams. If codes allow, attach plastic footing pads to the bottoms of the posts, and set them in the holes. Otherwise, pour in-ground or aboveground concrete footings, depending on local codes. Use your leveling system to mark all of the posts for cutting a beam's width below the bottom of the ledger. Cut the posts, and attach the beams on top.

Install the joist framing. At the angled bump-out, install joists that are longer than needed; brace them in position; and use a straightedge or chalk line to mark them for cutting to length. Add header joists.

Attach the railing posts to the inside of the framing. Add blocking to make the posts firm.

DECKING, FASCIA, AND RAILING. Install the decking, starting at the house and moving outward. Once the decking is installed, use a chalk line to mark for cutting straight lines that are 4 inches (10cm) from the edges of the framing. Cut the lines. Cut perimeter decking pieces to frame the deck, and install them. Add fascia pieces beneath the overhanging decking.

Railing like this is in kit form, with the balusters precut. Slip the sleeves over the 4x4 (10cmx10cm) posts. Cut the railing pieces to fit between the posts, and test the fit. Assemble each rail-and-baluster section, and attach it to the posts using the hardware provided.

STAIRS. Measure to determine how many steps you will need; estimate where the stringers will end; and pour or lay a concrete or paver landing pad. Cut and install the stringers. Dig postholes for the bottom railing posts, and set the posts in concrete for firmness. Add the treads and risers, then slip the post sleeves over the posts, and install the railings.

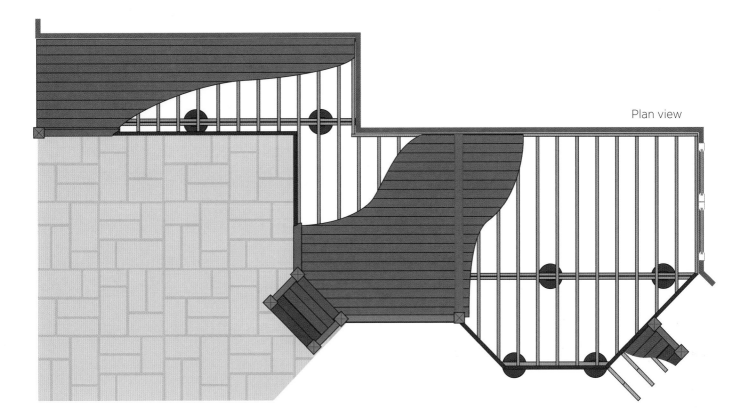

Plan view

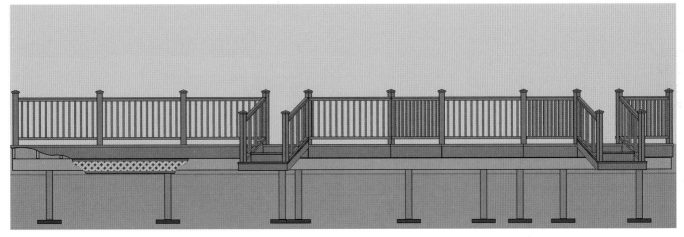

Elevation

MATERIALS

» **FRAMING**
- ❏ 6x6 (15cmx15cm) posts
- ❏ Metal 2x8 (5cmx20cm) joists, header, and ledger, with fastening hardware
- ❏ 4x8 (10cmx20cm) metal beams
- ❏ 2x12 (5cmx30cm) pressure-treated stair stringers

» **FOOTINGS**
- ❏ Plastic footing pads

» **DECKING AND FASCIA**
- ❏ 5/4x6 (3cmx15cm) composite decking
- ❏ Hidden fasteners
- ❏ 1x8 (2.5cmx20cm) fascia board
- ❏ Composite lattice sheets for skirting

» **RAILING**
- ❏ 4x4 (10cmx10cm) railing posts
- ❏ Composite railing system

Zigzag Charm

The charm of knotty wood decking and railings take center stage on this meandering deck. A series of partial octagons creates nooks and crannies as well as open space to make this a fun place for kids and adults alike.

The Design

The customers are grandparents who often take care of their grandchildren. They were looking for a safe, enclosed deck that would be spacious enough for hyperactive preschoolers to blow off steam, and at the same time comfortable and relaxing for adults. A large deck with four or five separate use areas offers a nice range of possibilities: adults can relax in their own space while children play nearby, and the children can choose between sand play, crafts, or active romping in an inviting fresh-air space.

SHAPE AND SIZE. The deck features three sections that are at least somewhat octagonal. At one end is a raised section, one step up from the rest of the deck, which actually *is* octagonal. Furnished with a small table and a few stuffed chairs, it serves as a homelike living room-type space. Though it is raised only 7½ inches (19.1cm), the slight elevation sets the area apart as special.

Seating area. The raised octagonal seating area framed with half-wide decking pieces has a satisfying shape and finished appearance. Trim pieces at the base of the fascia make it look like built-in baseboard molding.

Dining area. Purchased before the deck was built, a six-person table with chairs fits perfectly in the bumped-out section built to accommodate it.

Out-of-the-way grilling. Tucked away in a corner, the grill is out of the way of traffic and children's play zones.

A wide semi-octagonal bump-out in the dining area makes it possible to move the dining table away from the house a couple of feet (about 61cm), which frees up space for traffic flow and a grilling area. As he often does, de la Cruz designed this to suit the furniture: the bump-out is carefully placed where the dining table will be. Its shape—8 feet (2.5m) wide at the furthest point, with 2-foot-wide (61cm) "wings"—mirrors the traffic flow around the table-plus-chairs. The final partial octagon occurs at the other end of the deck, where it defines an activity center for children.

KID-FRIENDLY. One goal was to create a kid-friendly place. This is achieved in part simply by providing a large open area. Moving the dining table forward into an angled section opened up a space wide enough for big wheels and games of tag. A hinged gate at the top of the stairs makes the deck fully enclosed for safety.

The children's activity area, in the partial octagon at one end of the deck, currently features a standup sandbox. (A deck is a good place for sand play because sand overflow is easily swept between the decking joints.) This area could easily become an artist studio with an easel or a play table for crafts or water play. A play space on the deck lets kids be kids, with all the mess and noise that may entail, cheerfully absorbed in the great outdoors.

Kid-safe. A hinged gate at the top of the stairs makes the deck fully enclosed.

Activity space. A deck is an ideal place for messy kid activities. Wayward sand will fall or can easily be swept through the cracks.

Solid skirting. Decking pieces with ⅛-inch (0.3cm) gaps between them are installed as solid skirting. Gus builds a solid frame for the skirt, so it does not wobble when bumped. Still, he prefers to have a gravel edge so that the lawn mower will not come near the wood.

Railing touches. Though made of casual-looking knotty wood, the railing design looks neat and finished because it features classic post caps and a fastening system that hides screw heads.

Fastener details. In some places, visible fastener heads are unavoidable, so finish nails and small-headed screws were used.

Decking pattern. Angled decking that meets at a central divider strip adds style and definition to the floor plan—and eliminates the need for butt joints.

MATERIALS. The surprise here is that this deck is made of all pressure-treated lumber—but of a somewhat unusual type. Today's common wood treatments are generally considered safe, but de la Cruz went one step further, using lumber with a treatment that does not include copper or other metals, so is even safer for small children, even if they chew on it.

The lumber is rated at No. 1, or "premium," with only small, tight knots. The pressure treatment, produced by the Eco-Life company, not only is safe but also includes additives that stop cracking. (See the Resource Guide,

page 216.) If you look carefully at the deck, you will have a hard time finding any of the visible cracks or other blemishes that often mar the appearance of a treated deck. In addition, de la Cruz used hidden fasteners on the deck and designed and built the railing to show a minimal number of screw heads; you can see them only where the rails attach to the posts. These screws have small heads, so they burrow into the wood and become almost invisible. The skirting is the only place where fastener heads are more visible.

Building the Deck

When building a wood deck, carefully choose boards that are dry, straight, and free of large knots or other blemishes. You will build the basic deck framing first, then the raised octagonal section.

FRAMING. Install the ledger, 2½ inches (6.5cm) below the house's threshold, to make the finished deck surface 1½ inches (4cm) below the threshold. Use fasteners and flashing as required by codes.

Dig straight lines of postholes to support the two long beams. If codes allow, attach plastic footing pads to the bottoms of posts and set them in the holes. Otherwise, pour in-ground or aboveground concrete footings, depending on local codes. Hold the posts in place with temporary supports. Use a transit or a level atop a long board to mark the posts for cutting a beam's width below the bottom of the ledger. Cut the posts; build the beams; and attach the beams on top of the posts, using code-approved hardware.

Install the joist framing. Because the deck is wider than 20 feet (6.1m), you will need two lengths of joists. Install the first joists so that they slightly overhang the first post, with joist hangers at the ledger. Install joists and blocking where the decking divider strip will be, as shown in the illustration on page 141. Add the second section of joists, and fasten them to the sides of the first section. At the angled bump-out, install joists that are longer than needed; brace them in position; and use a straightedge or chalk line to mark them for cutting to length. Add header joists.

Build framing for the octagonal section on top of the main framing. Dig postholes; install posts; and install three short beams to support the octagon where it does not rest on the deck.

Attach the railing posts to the inside of the framing; then add blocking to make the posts firm.

DECKING, FASCIA, AND RAILING. Cut decking ends at 45 degrees, and install the angled decking. Install one section with boards that overhang the divider-strip framing. Mark their tops with a chalk line that is 90 degrees to the house, and cut the line. Install the other side, longer than it needs to be, with angled cuts on each side. Make another chalk-line cut that is one decking board's width plus ¼ inch (0.5cm) for joints on each side. Then install the divider strip. Once the decking is installed, use a chalk line to mark for cutting straight lines that are 4 inches (10cm) from the edges of the framing. Cut the lines. Cut pieces of perimeter decking to frame the deck, and install them. Add fascia pieces under the overhanging decking.

Build the railing in sections that fit between posts. Cut the top and bottom rails, plus a 2x2 (5cmx5cm) nailer. Mark the bottom rail and the nailer for evenly spaced 2x2 (5cmx5cm) balusters. Working on a flat surface, attach the balusters to the bottom rails and the nailer using screws. Attach the 2x4 (5cmx10cm) top rail to the top of the nailer by driving screws up, so they won't be visible. Attach the sections to the posts with angle-driven screws. Add decorative post caps and trim pieces.

MATERIALS

» **FRAMING (ALL TREATED)**
- ☐ 6x6 (15cmx15cm) posts
- ☐ 2x8 (5cmx20cm) joists, header, and ledger, with fastening hardware
- ☐ 2x8s (5cmx20cm) for beams
- ☐ 2x12 (5cmx30cm) stair stringers

» **FOOTINGS**
- ☐ Plastic footing pads or concrete

» **DECKING AND FASCIA**
- ☐ 5/4x6 (3cmx15cm) pressure-treated decking, using an eco-friendly treatment
- ☐ Hidden fasteners
- ☐ 1x8 (2.5cmx20cm) fascia board
- ☐ 2x4s (5cmx10cm) to frame for skirting
- ☐ Decking pieces for skirting

» **RAILING (ALL TREATED)**
- ☐ 4x4 (10cmx10cm) posts
- ☐ 2x4 (5cmx10cm) top and bottom rails
- ☐ 2x2 (5cmx5cm) balusters
- ☐ Decorative post caps
- ☐ Trim for top and bottom of posts

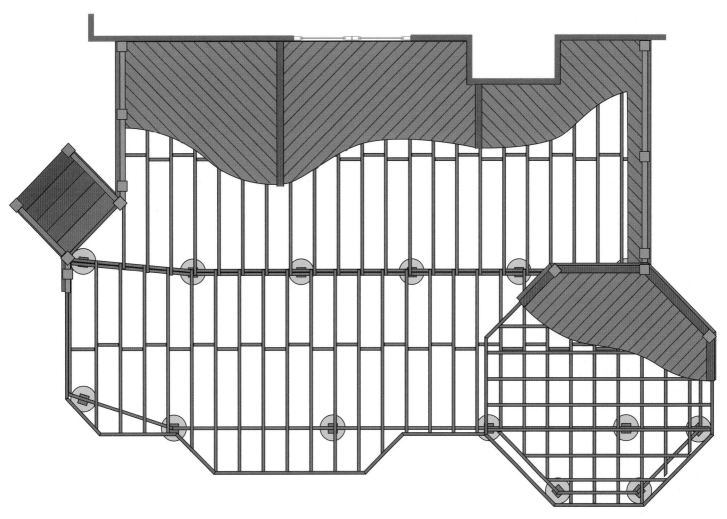

Plan view

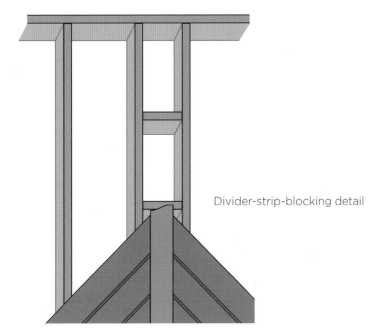

Divider-strip-blocking detail

Half Circle with Wings

A central semicircular dining area, flanked by two long sections, one an outdoor kitchen and the other an informal conversation area, anchors this lovely raised design. The gray composite decking and white bead-board trim suggest the Cape Cod style.

The Design

The owners felt that the back of the house was a bit plain looking and needed some "style-bumping." Gus suggested a semicircular area, and they instantly loved the idea. An outdoor kitchen was a priority, so space was reserved for that. They also wanted their kids to feel free to play on the deck; it was designed to include a 40-foot-long (12.2m) runway for big wheels.

OVERALL DESIGN. There are three main sections, plus a couple of small nooks. At one end, an outdoor kitchen replaces the railing. The semicircular section is 20 feet (6.1m) in diameter, so it can handle even a very large dining table. At the other end is a conversation section, with chairs and a circular table. The table includes a fire pit, making it a favorite nighttime gathering spot.

MATERIALS. High-quality composite decking and PVC railing ensure that the deck will be easy to clean for many decades. There are no nearby trees, so the deck is exposed to bright sunlight much of the time. The light gray color, a somewhat unusual choice, reflects much of the sunlight and radiant heat, so the deck does not get too warm in the summer. It also coordinates beautifully with the house's white siding and black roofing shingles. The faux wood grain looks like wood that has been coated with solid stain.

The railing is made from white vinyl posts and rails with black metal balusters—in keeping with a black-and-white palette.

OUTDOOR KITCHEN. The L-shape outdoor kitchen is just a few steps away from the indoor kitchen and about 8 feet (2.5m) away from the dining table—far enough so that grilling smoke will not bother diners. The countertop is granite with a short backsplash, so things cannot slide off and fall to the ground behind. There is a long countertop to the right of the grill and a 16-inch-long (40.6cm) section

Simple seating. A reading area need not take up a lot of space.

Water feature. An electric-powered fountain ringed with potted plants adds a spark of life and color.

on its left—large enough for a plate of meat. The kitchen features a large gas grill with doors for storage, as well as small refrigerator. An opening under the countertop is just the right size for garbage and recycling bins, and two recessed areas hold grilling utensils (on one side) and miscellaneous accessories (on the other).

Sound framing. The structural composite-lumber beam is stronger than even two 2x12s (5cmx30cm) and so decreases the required number of support posts under the deck.

Fire pit. A rectangular area at the far end of the deck includes a table with a gas fire pit for evening conversation, sing-alongs, or activities like roasting hot dogs and s'mores.

Personalized details. When the concrete landing pad at the bottom of the stairs was poured, the owners made sure the kids were on hand to lend their impressions.

Spacious kitchen. The outdoor kitchen has plenty of counter space, room for garbage and utensil storage, and a handy little refrigerator.

Building the Deck

Use high-quality treated lumber for the framing. To minimize the number of posts under the deck, use structural composite lumber (also called engineered beams) approved by local codes. Installing curved decking and railing calls for special equipment; see page 130–131 for more information.

FRAMING. Attach a ledger using code-approved flashing. Build joist framing by attaching the joists to the ledger using joist hangers and holding up the other end with temporary supports. Cut the joists, and install the straight headers.

Where the curve will be, run the joists longer than required. Install blocking to make sure all of the joists are correctly spaced. Make a long string-and-pencil compass to mark the tops of the joists at the curved sections. Mark each side of each joist for end cuts, and adjust the circular saw slightly for each cut.

To make the curved header, cut strips of pressure-treated plywood the same width as the joists. Attach the plywood to the ends of the joists. Cut the pieces so that joints occur at the middles of joists. Install three layers of plywood, offsetting the joints from layer to layer.

Where the beams will go, dig straight rows of postholes. Attach the engineered beams to the underside of the joists, above the holes. Pour concrete into the holes as required by code, or use plastic post footings. Set the posts; cut them to height; and attach them to the underside of the beams.

Run natural gas (if not using propane) and electrical lines for the outdoor kitchen, deck lighting, and ceiling lights for the roof.

DECKING AND RAILING. Install the 4x4 (10cmx10cm) railing posts, attached to the inside of the framing with blocking as shown in the illustration on page 145.

To bend composite decking, see pages 130–131. Follow instructions on pages 80–81 for installing the curved decking.

Install the PVC post sleeves over the railing posts. Use the same forms as you used for the curved decking pieces to curve the railing pieces. Cut the railing pieces to length so that they fit between the posts. Assemble the rails with the balusters; then attach the sections to the posts using the hardware provided.

Install PVC fascia under the decking. Attach treads to the stair stringers, and add fascia boards as the risers. For the small landing on the lower level, build a simple 2x8 (5cmx20cm) frame, and cover it with decking and fascia.

OUTDOOR KITCHEN. Build the outdoor kitchen by making cabinets of PVC sheets. Add a granite countertop, and install the grill and refrigerator. (See Creative Homeowner's *Building Outdoor Kitchens for Every Budget* for full instructions.)

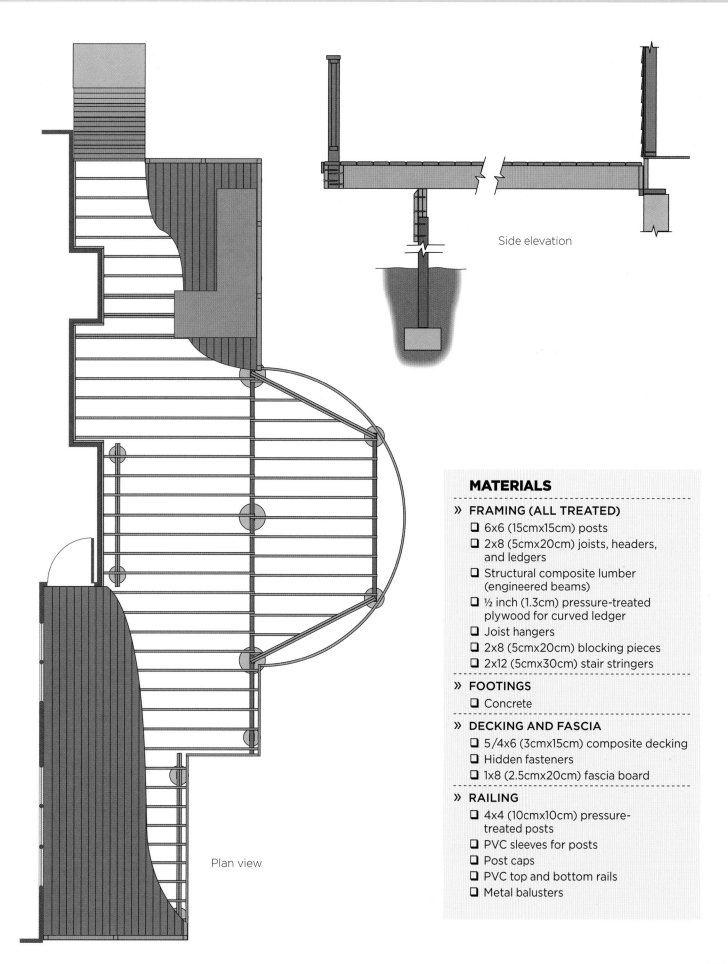

Side elevation

Plan view

MATERIALS

» FRAMING (ALL TREATED)
- ❑ 6x6 (15cmx15cm) posts
- ❑ 2x8 (5cmx20cm) joists, headers, and ledgers
- ❑ Structural composite lumber (engineered beams)
- ❑ ½ inch (1.3cm) pressure-treated plywood for curved ledger
- ❑ Joist hangers
- ❑ 2x8 (5cmx20cm) blocking pieces
- ❑ 2x12 (5cmx30cm) stair stringers

» FOOTINGS
- ❑ Concrete

» DECKING AND FASCIA
- ❑ 5/4x6 (3cmx15cm) composite decking
- ❑ Hidden fasteners
- ❑ 1x8 (2.5cmx20cm) fascia board

» RAILING
- ❑ 4x4 (10cmx10cm) pressure-treated posts
- ❑ PVC sleeves for posts
- ❑ Post caps
- ❑ PVC top and bottom rails
- ❑ Metal balusters

Rolling Ridge Deck and Outdoor Living

Barry Streett has been building decks for about 25 years, starting in Maryland and then moving to Colorado in 1995. He and his company have built more than a thousand decks in that time.

Streett long ago decided to work at the high end of the design and skill scale. He prides himself in doing work that other builders cannot do, and feels that he can meet the needs and fulfill the desires of the most exacting customers.

Many homes in his part of Colorado are on steep sites, which means that they do not have usable backyards. So his decks often effectively take the place of a backyard. Customers often want large decks; 800 square feet is an average size.

Natural elements. Barry's designs often incorporate stone and brick elements, which contrast beautifully with decking materials. The fireplace in the foreground and the kitchen counter in the background are designed and built to minimize the chance that sparks can land on the decking.

Barry Streett

ROLLING RIDGE DECK AND OUTDOOR LIVING COMPANY

Evergreen, Colorado
303-670-4919
rollingridgedeck.com

THE DESIGN PROCESS

Streett begins by going through a customer's wants and needs and then addresses those needs by designing a deck with suitable rooms. The idea is to bring interior rooms—a living room, dining room, kitchen, or spa—to the outside.

His first goal is to provide the right amount of functional space. Although his decks are usually large, he urges his customers to develop a plan so that each section has a purpose and no space is wasted.

To get an idea of how a future deck will look and feel, builders often have homeowners place lawn furniture outside, on the site. Streett, however, believes that this method makes a deck seem smaller than it really will be, so he usually lays out portions of the deck inside the house for a more accurate sense of the space. He uses outdoor furniture, and designs rooms that fit around the pieces.

Streett aims to build decks that respect the architecture of the house. He wants his decks to look as if they really belong rather than being tacked on. In his area of Colorado, houses are often rustic or cabin-like in appearance, and many of his decks feature log railings and other rough-hewn features. For a house that is more modern or refined, he chooses materials to complete the look and contribute to the style.

OUTDOOR KITCHENS AND FIREPLACES

About 95 percent of Streett's customers want an outdoor kitchen and/or fireplace on their deck. A fireplace is usually a large, maybe even imposing structure, so he typically makes it a focal point. And because a fireplace is an important architectural feature, Streett makes sure that the home's exterior and other architectural features provide context for the design. A well-chosen location on the deck can also provide practical benefits: a fireplace can block an undesirable view, for instance, or provide privacy by blocking a neighbor's view.

Exceptional engineering. A graceful curved stairway like this is a real construction challenge, executed brilliantly by Streett.

Porch space. Many of Streett's decks include covered porch areas. Here, a vaulting bead-board-and-timber ceiling provides cover for a full-service outdoor kitchen.

Overhead shade. Sun shining through a pergola creates partial shade with a playful pattern of light for this spa and lounging area.

Organic curves. This custom iron railing follows a gentle perimeter curve, while the sharper curve in the foreground defines two deck levels. The deck-level curve is not a circular radius, which makes it organic rather than geometric.

Spa accommodations. This spa is accessible from two sides and two levels, so bathers have comfortable options for entering and exiting.

Decorative additions. This narrow rough-timber pergola against the house is mostly decorative but also provides welcome shade when the sun is high.

Freestanding structure. This freestanding destination deck, seen from two perspectives, enjoys natural shade and a glorious view of the Rocky Mountains.

Natural features. Streett often combines masonry and decking, creating a deck that feels anchored to the stony landscape.

Tied to the landscape. Meticulously curve-cut decking accommodates surrounding boulders, blurring the line between manmade and natural.

RAILINGS AND CURVES

Streett believes that the railing is the most important visual element of a deck and, in fact, is often what makes a deck special. So he offers a nearly limitless range of railing options, from log construction to composites with side-mounted metal balusters to custom iron railings. He also designs custom iron railings himself; see "Railings to Choose, page 158–159, for examples. Views are important to many of Streett's customers, so most of his railings are as open as possible. His custom iron railings normally have thin balusters that barely inhibit enjoyment of the mountain view.

Like other high-end builders, Streett often builds decks with curved decking and railings; in fact, nearly all his decks have curves. He takes sinuous lines to new levels with projects that curve in several directions. And some of his curves are not simple radii; they snake naturally with changing arcs along their length as if to mold the deck to the surrounding mountain setting.

Streett's Techniques

1 Streett enjoys difficult engineering challenges—feats like building on severe slopes, creating elaborate curves, and building decks elevated more than 20 feet (6.1m).

2 To create custom metal railings, he first designs them himself and then has a metalworking partner make the railings to fit. A strong powder coating is applied for great protection against rust. It is important to use a reputable and experienced fabricator and powder-coater to ensure that the rails are solid and last a very long time.

3 Streett often uses large engineered beams—cedar exterior glue-laminated beams, for instance—which span longer distances because they are stronger than the usual doubled 2-bys (5cm-bys). This enables him to be a minimalist below the deck. The fewer the posts, the more pristine the deck looks from the outside. (Cedar glue-laminated beams might not be approved in wetter climates; there, pressure-treated beams are often required.)

4 For joists and beams, he uses the best lumber: No. 1 southern yellow pine kiln-dried after treatment (KDAT). It is worth the extra cost because it is so stable and straight.

5 He also sometimes builds with steel framing, which produces perfectly flat deck surfaces with fewer beams. He prefers to use "G90" galvanized joists rather than the usual "G60" because they are stronger. In his dry climate, powder-coating the joists is not needed.

6 Streett's footings are often extra heavy duty, especially when supporting high decks with few posts. This means digging to below the frost line or, better yet, to bedrock and pouring steel-reinforced concrete columns that rise 8 inches (20.3cm) or so above grade. In his dry climate, he can install non-treated Douglas fir posts. In looser soil, he often installs massive helical piers, which are actually screwed into the ground with special equipment.

7 Streett does not like the look of exposed decking ends; he prefers a cleaner appearance. So he usually cuts decking flush with outside joists, then installs the fascia so that its top edge is flush with the top of the decking. This method works well for high-quality composite materials but is not recommended for wood decking or lesser-quality composites, which may warp, leading to unsightly gaps between decking and fascia.

8 Although Streett's decks are by no means inexpensive, he is opposed to wasteful spending. He tends to "value engineer" when designing, meaning that he may change the size or shape of a deck to save a significant amount of money. A 16-foot (4.9m) framing expanse may cost a great deal more than a 14-foot (4.3m) one, for example, so he may encourage the customer to go with a slightly narrower deck.

Log Cabin Chic

This deck packs a lot of outdoor living options into a comparatively modest space—and it all fits beautifully, with no wasted space. Log railings, together with a few additional log features, tie it all together.

The Design

The owners had a long wish list: an outdoor kitchen with lots of features, a dining area, and a fireplace with wide-open seating facing it. A larger deck could have been built, but it would have looked out of scale with the medium-size house. So Streett designed carefully.

The outdoor kitchen is just out the door from the house's kitchen. The dining area, off to the side on its own lower level (barely visible at left in the side-view photo), has room for a round table for four or six plus some potted plants.

LOGS. The log railing system, produced by a local fabricator, is a sentimental favorite in Colorado. It is made of lodgepole pine, which has a natural honey color and is prone to rustic cracks and splits. Less-expensive log structures have the bark peeled by machine, resulting in a mostly smooth surface that has been called "semi-rustic." The more expensive method, used here, removes the bark by hand with an old-fashioned drawknife. The result is a more authentic pioneer look. Rails and balusters are hand-cut to fit into holes, and the resulting imperfections are all part of the charm.

Streett normally discourages buyers from purchasing log railings because they typically last only about 10 years and then need to be replaced. He builds in such a way that replacement can be done without dismantling the whole deck, but it is still an expensive proposition. Some homeowners love the logs so much, though, that they are willing to pay for replacement down the line.

FITTING IN. The house itself is standard horizontal siding with plain trim and no rustic features. To help tie things together so that the new rough-hewn railings would fit with the house, Streett made a couple of alterations. He framed the house's door with poles in a simple post-and-lintel arrangement. This framing is simply ornamental; the door's original trim is left in place and simply covered by logs. And when building the deck, he applied cedar trim to match the color of the house trim; it can be seen on the deck's fascia and the fireplace roof. Small complements like this go a long way toward pulling together two different styles.

Log rails and balusters. Rails and balusters are carved to fit into holes. Some gaps are filled with chinking, which can be stained to nearly match the color of the logs.

Living room. The kitchen area opens to the large hexagonal living room with plenty of space to stretch out by the fireplace.

Log posts. The logs are notched so that framing can be securely attached. Most log posts rest on aboveground concrete footings, but some are attached to the deck. The two at the bottom of the stairway are sunk belowground into concrete for added stiffness.

Countertop details. The slate tiles used in the countertop are small enough that they might be considered mosaics. The overhang makes for a friendly eating surface near the cook.

FIREPLACE AND OUTDOOR KITCHEN. The outdoor living room faces the fireplace, which is the deck's focal point. Because the fireplace is gas-fired, it does not need a chimney, stays clean looking, and does not produce smoke. It is housed in a structure that is covered with natural "thin stone."

The spacious L-shape kitchen features a large high-end grill, together with a refrigerator and matching stainless-steel doors for access to storage underneath. The counter siding incorporates the same stone as the fireplace. The two-level countertop, made of small slate tiles, has a decorative diamond pattern along the edging. The work surface is 36 inches (91cm) tall, while a snacking/bar surface is 42 inches (1.1m) tall with an overhang to accommodate bar stools.

Fireplace. The fireplace, faced in natural stone, has a seating area by the hearth. This gas unit is insulated and designed to be safe to install with wood surfaces nearby.

Building the Deck

The log railing posts are part of the structure, supporting the outer flush beam. There is a center drop beam for the larger deck. Build the framing on temporary supports; then install the footings, posts, and interior drop beam.

FRAMING. Install the ledgers with flashing at the house for the two deck levels. [The lower level uses 2x10 (5cmx25cm) framing because it has no center beam.] Where the center beam will be, dig a straight row of footing holes, pour concrete into forms, and install the support posts with temporary bracing. Use a level or transit to mark the post heights, and cut them one beam's width lower than the bottom of the ledger. Assemble the beam of three 2x10s (5cmx25cm), and set the beam on top of the posts.

Attach the joists to the ledger using joist hangers, and rest them on the beam or a temporary support. On the wider deck area, the joists split on the beam. Install blocking as required. Use a chalk line and square to mark the joists for cutting at the ends, and cut them using a circular saw. Attach two or three layers of 2x10s (5cmx25cm) to the joist ends to make a flush beam.

RAILING. Dig postholes for the combination railing and structural posts, and pour concrete footings with code-approved hardware for securing the post bottoms. Use a small chain saw to notch the posts so they will fit flat against the flush beam. Check with a string line to be sure that the posts form straight lines.

Assemble the balustrades, and attach them to the posts. Slip the posts onto the mounting hardware; press the posts against the flush beam; and drive long screws through the beam and into the posts. Cut a channel in the back of each post where post lights will go; run the wiring; and then fill the channel with chinking.

FIREPLACE AND OUTDOOR KITCHEN. The fireplace is a metal gas-fired unit. Follow instructions for running natural gas and electrical lines to it. Install the unit, and surround it with framed plywood. Cover the plywood with roofing felt, wire lath, and mortar; then apply the stone facing. Fill the joints between the stones with mortar. Build the roof with plywood, roofing felt, and shingles, and add a simple log structure to hold up its ends.

Make the outdoor kitchen counter using wood or metal studs, cement-based backer board, and stone facing. For the countertop, make the substrate out of two layers of backer board. Tiled outdoor countertop surfaces often fail, but yours can last if you use the right products: set the tiles in high-quality polymer-reinforced thin-set mortar or epoxy resin mortar. Fill the joints with epoxy grout. (For more instructions on building an outdoor kitchen counter, see Creative Homeowner's *Building Outdoor Kitchens for Every Budget*.)

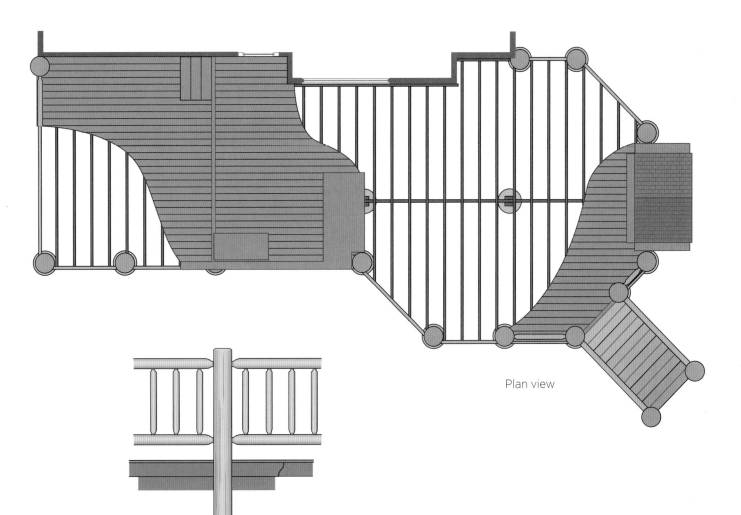

Plan view

Elevation

MATERIALS

» FRAMING (ALL TREATED)
- ❑ 6x6 (15cmx15cm) posts
- ❑ 2x8 (5cmx20cm) and 2x10 (5cmx25cm) joists, headers, and ledgers
- ❑ 2x10s (5cmx25cm), tripled for beams
- ❑ Joist hangers
- ❑ 2x8 (5cmx20cm) blocking pieces
- ❑ 2x12 (5cmx30cm) stair stringers
- ❑ Footings

» CONCRETE AND FORMS
- ❑ Anchoring hardware for bottom of log posts

» DECKING AND FASCIA
- ❑ 5/4x6 (3cmx15cm) composite decking
- ❑ Hidden fasteners
- ❑ 1x10 (2.5cmx25cm) cedar fascia

» RAILING
- ❑ 10 inch (25.4cm) log posts
- ❑ Log rails and balusters
- ❑ Stainable chinking
- ❑ Long screws for attaching to framing

Railings to Choose

The railings are the jewels in almost any deck design. And Streett ensures that they will last as long as possible by carefully protecting them against rust and rot. He will either cover them with a solid powder coating or use composite or wood materials that are sure not to rot. Railings should be installed to precisely follow the deck's contours, which is especially difficult when it comes to curves.

This all-metal black-coated railing has stylish balusters with provocative curves.

The simple geometry of straight balusters and rails neatly complements the clean lines of this deck.

Every third baluster in this railing has a decorative flourish at its center, adding understated ornamentation.

This curved iron rail, powder-coated in a color to blend with the decking, features a double top rail and diamond-shape openings.

Rustic rough-hewn railings impart log cabin charm.

Even if the decking is composite, many homeowners prefer natural wood for the railing—the portion of the deck that is most handled and looked at up close.

Massive cedar railing posts with painted metal caps stand like stately sentries holding the iron railing system in place.

Wavy balusters and a curlicue detail in the center dress up this gate.

This iron railing is fully dressed up with stone-faced-and-capped columns with post lights plus an ipé top cap.

Many people prefer to top a metal railing with a cap made of composite or wood. The cap can support small potted plants and is a bit more comfortable to lean on.

Curved This Way, Then That

This deck describes a meandering path around the house to an entry door on the side. Most curves bulge outward from the house, but one curves inward to add complexity. Stone facing at the base of the house and the deck helps tie everything together because the stone colors blend well with the composite decking and fascia. The stone makes the deck feel solid but also a bit fanciful, like an old castle.

The Design

The owners wanted a deck that made a stunning design statement, and they wanted it to fit with the house's architecture. A large curved section on the back of the house set the stage. The deck, divided into two sections, supplies room for all of the most popular activities: cooking, dining, lounging, and soaking in a spa. An adjacent patio includes a fire pit to complete the options.

SHAPE AND SIZE. The house's rear wall does not have a back door, so entry is from the side (just out of view to the right). A short walkway from the door leads to the largest deck area, with a wide curved prow facing the backyard. There is no dedicated outdoor kitchen, but near the house there is ample room for a portable grill in addition to the dining table. (If winds are blowing toward the dining table, the homeowners can easily wheel the grill farther away.) Because the curved section is free of furniture, it feels a little like a balcony and is perfect for standing and enjoying the view.

An arcing 5-foot-wide (1.5m) walkway leads to a smaller area dedicated to soaking. The spa's top edge is about a foot (30.5cm) above the deck surface; stairs on each side and a set of deck steps in front make it easy for people of all sizes to enter and exit.

The deck's multiple curves are not symmetrical. Streett takes an organic approach and does not simply use radii. If you follow the perimeter line that is parallel with the house, you will see a variety of curves. The largest curve is not actually a partial circle; it straightens out slightly at the left side (as you look at it). And the wide stairs are slightly flatter than the curve of the deck at their top landing. Add to this the flowing curves of the concrete patio, and you have a deck with graceful aesthetic appeal.

MATERIALS. The decking and railing are made of top-quality composite lumber, which will stay colorfast and easy to clean for a very long time. The patio, made of concrete that is stamped, stained, and sealed, is also low maintenance. The stonework of the deck, which matches that of the house, is a natural "thin stone" rather than faux stone.

Spa seating. Positioned between two sets of cascading stairs—always popular sitting spaces—this spa has easy access for soakers of any size. The nearby lounge chair is a comfortable place to dry out (or cool off).

Quality joinery. Tight, consistent joinery makes this deck a pleasure to use. Stair treads cannot be attached using hidden fasteners, so Streett used discretely colored screws instead.

Railing detail. The stair railing includes a graspable element, made of a piece of decking with a routed groove on each side, attached on end to the inside of the top rail.

Curved stairs. Wide, curving stairs with lights in the risers provide inviting seating during large gatherings.

Building the Deck

This spa is supported by deck framing, but your codes may require pouring a concrete slab for support. To install the drop beam for a low deck, you may need to excavate to a depth of a foot (30.5cm) or so. Streett built the deck first, then had masonry for the patio poured up to it, but you may choose to install the concrete patio first.

START FRAMING. Install the ledger 2½ inches (6.5cm) below the house's threshold. Dig straight rows of footing holes for the beams near the house. Install the support posts according to local codes, and cut them to height, one beam's width below the bottom of the ledger. Build and attach the beam. Install the joists running from the ledger to the beam so that they overhang the beam slightly.

Install the joists—longer than they need to be—farther away from the house so that they rest on the first beam and on temporary supports at the end. Install blocking, and make sure that the joists are positioned correctly; then mark their tops for end cuts.

FRAMING CURVES. To mark the joists for cutting on a curve, start with a string-and-pencil compass to get some basic curves. Then, for more refined and complex curves, work visually. Streett says that this is where the *art* comes in, so take your time. Use a piece of ⅜-inch (1cm) flexible copper tubing or a fascia board to lay out for the S-curves and places where a radius gets modified. Stand back; look at the curves; and make modifications until you are satisfied.

Cut the joists to length; you will need to adjust your circular saw's bevel slightly for each cut. Add a built-up flush beam using plywood, as discussed on pages 128–129. Dig holes; pour footings; install and cut support posts; and install the outer drop beams. If required, install rows of blocking.

Determine where the stairs will end, using the same technique for figuring curves. Pour the concrete footing (for the single bottom railing post); install the stringers; and install the post.

CURVED WALL. The illustration page 163 shows framing and sheathing for the curved wall. Once the framing is done, pour a concrete footing directly below the curved header. Cut a bottom plate out of a piece of 2x12 (5cmx30cm) so it is 3½ inches (8.9cm) wide, to follow the curve of the header. Attach the plate to the concrete, and install 2x4 (5cmx10cm) studs every 16 inches (40.6cm). Attach treated plywood to the studs. After you have finished decking (next paragraph), you will install the fascia. Then you will staple roofing felt and metal lath onto the plywood, trowel on a layer of mortar, and install the facing stones.

DECKING AND RAILING. Install wood railing posts against the header joists. Install decking using hidden fasteners; use colored face screws where needed for the stair treads. At the curves, install the decking so that it overhangs; then carefully curve-cut the decking flush to the outside of the headers. Add fascia so that it comes up flush with the top of the decking. To bend the stair treads, use a heating system. (See pages 130–131.)

Notch the post sleeves as needed, and slip them over the railing posts. Assemble rail-and-baluster sections to fit between the posts, and install using the hardware provided. Cap the railing with pieces of decking.

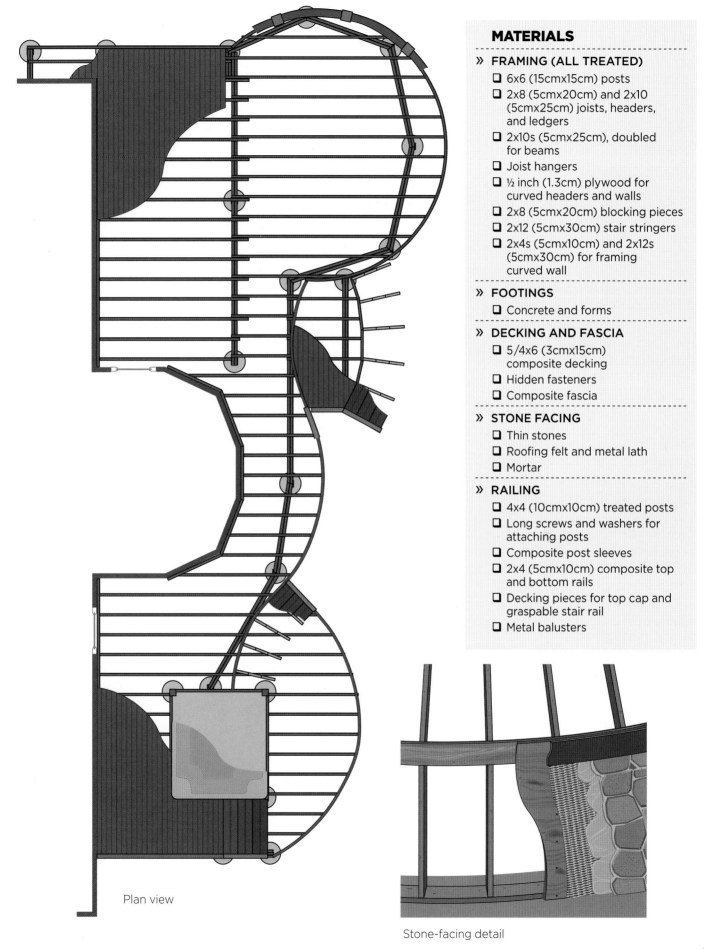

Plan view

MATERIALS

» **FRAMING (ALL TREATED)**
- ❑ 6x6 (15cmx15cm) posts
- ❑ 2x8 (5cmx20cm) and 2x10 (5cmx25cm) joists, headers, and ledgers
- ❑ 2x10s (5cmx25cm), doubled for beams
- ❑ Joist hangers
- ❑ ½ inch (1.3cm) plywood for curved headers and walls
- ❑ 2x8 (5cmx20cm) blocking pieces
- ❑ 2x12 (5cmx30cm) stair stringers
- ❑ 2x4s (5cmx10cm) and 2x12s (5cmx30cm) for framing curved wall

» **FOOTINGS**
- ❑ Concrete and forms

» **DECKING AND FASCIA**
- ❑ 5/4x6 (3cmx15cm) composite decking
- ❑ Hidden fasteners
- ❑ Composite fascia

» **STONE FACING**
- ❑ Thin stones
- ❑ Roofing felt and metal lath
- ❑ Mortar

» **RAILING**
- ❑ 4x4 (10cmx10cm) treated posts
- ❑ Long screws and washers for attaching posts
- ❑ Composite post sleeves
- ❑ 2x4 (5cmx10cm) composite top and bottom rails
- ❑ Decking pieces for top cap and graspable stair rail
- ❑ Metal balusters

Stone-facing detail

163

Scallops and Curves

This soaring deck nimbly wraps around the house on three sides. On its outer perimeter there is nary a straight line, and no curve is like another. The distinctive custom-built curved stairway adds flourish.

The Design

The owners were tired and bored with their existing quadrilateral deck and wanted something special. Streett came through with flying colors, crafting a one-of-a-kind deck with unique crescent contours.

HIGH DECK. The deck is about 12 feet (3.7m) aboveground. Streett installed an under-deck drainage system, with a gutter and downspout tucked away behind the beam. This keeps the space below dry, so it can be used as a sheltered porch/patio.

The tall structural posts are made of treated Douglas fir, a material that is extremely stable but exhibits a pattern of incisions required for the treatment process. To make the space below more attractive, Streett stained the posts. He also clad the beams with fascia boards and covered the undersides of the joists with plywood panels to create a ceiling. After the patio was installed, he clad the bottom 4 feet (1.2m) of the support posts with stonework.

THE CURVES. The deck is made with multiple curves. Looking from right to left (as you view the deck from the outside), there are two scallops reminiscent of the top of a heart shape. Continuing on, the curve becomes progressively flatter, until it forms an S-shape and turns the other way at the house's corner.

A bench snugs up to the railing at the second scallop. Recent code changes in some areas no longer allow you to put a bench next to a railing because children might stand on the bench and climb over the rail; check your local building codes to be sure.

Curved railings like this, which follow the contours of the deck precisely, call for first-rate workmanship and professional-level tools.

THE STAIRWAY. It is common for an upper deck to have an all-metal spiral stairway, which can be purchased as a kit. This stairway is much more ambitious because it is made of decking material and follows the curve of the deck. Streett had to build the stair stringers in place, a painstaking process.

LAYOUT. The homeowners can get access to the deck from inside the house via two sliding doors. The grill area is near the kitchen door in the first scallop, for convenience. A fire-pit area, suitable for buffet dining or just creating a convivial atmosphere, occupies the second scallop, and the dining table fits nicely in the large area to the left. There is room for a lounge chair near the dining table. Tucked away at the end of the deck, around the corner, is a private area for relaxing or sunning, big enough to accommodate several recliners and a small table.

Fire pit. A gas fire pit placed about 2 feet (61cm) from the built-in bench adds a warm glow to this spacious circular seating area.

Private lounging. A lounge area nestled in a corner is private but has a view of part of the deck; the curved shape defines the area.

Dining area. The dining table is well away from grilling smoke but easily accessible to the house via a sliding door.

Unique shapes. Meticulous details shine through in Streett's construction and elevate the overall appearance of the deck, as seen here in the winding stairway and arcing railings. The two scallops on the railing look like the top of a heart shape.

Stair construction. The stairway's stringers attach to the sides of the inside posts, and the railing butts the posts—requiring careful joinery. The outside railing has a graspable handrail made from a piece of decking with routed grooves, installed on end.

Curving stairs. The stairway gently and artfully curves down to the ground, delivering travelers to a landing beneath the deck.

Building the Deck

Building a second-story deck is a challenging project that requires the skills of experienced builders. Take plenty of safety precautions when working high.

FRAMING WITH CURVES. Install the ledger against the house using code-approved flashing and strong fasteners. Dig rows of postholes to nearly follow the contours of the deck; pour code-approved footings; and install support posts taller than they will be, temporarily bracing them in position. (Alternatively, build the joist framing on temporary supports, and install the beam, posts, and footings later.) Use a transit to mark the posts for cutting to height, one beam's width below the bottom of the ledger. Build the beams, and attach them to the tops of the support posts using code-approved hardware. [On this deck, most of the beams are double 2x10s (5cmx25cm), but for the beam with longer runs between supports posts, triple 2x10s (5cmx25cm) were required.]

Temporarily but firmly brace the posts and beams, using 2x6 (5cmx15cm) braces and long stakes. Attach the joists to the ledger using joist hangers. Allow them to run past the beams. Attach them to the beams, correctly spaced, and use bracing as needed to hold them firmly in place. To mark the tops of the joists for cutting on a curve, use a string-and-pencil compass to get a general idea; then use ⅜-inch (1cm) flexible copper tubing or a piece of composite fascia to lay out the final curves. Take your time, and stand back to examine the curves until you are satisfied. Cut the joists to length; you will need to adjust your circular saw's bevel slightly for each cut. Install curved headers made out of plywood.

If you will build a curved bench, install simple framing of paired 4x4 (10cmx10cm) posts that follow the deck's curve. Install blocking as needed to keep the posts firm.

Install an under-deck drainage system, with gutters and downspouts as needed.

DECKING AND FASCIA. You may choose to install the decking and railing first, then the curved stairs, or build the curved stairs first. Here, we show the decking first. Attach 4x4 (10cmx10cm) posts to the outsides of the headers. Install composite decking using hidden fasteners. At the curves, install the decking so that it overhangs; then carefully curve-cut it flush to the outside of the headers. Add fascia boards so that their tops are flush with the decking surface.

Notch post sleeves as needed, and slip them over the 4x4 (10cmx10cm) posts. Use a heating system to bend the top and bottom rails, as well as the top cap, so they follow the deck's contours. Cut the pieces so they fit between the posts. Build sections of rails and balusters, and attach them between the posts. Add the top cap, made of bent decking.

STAIRWAY. Build the stringers for the curved stairway in place. Install the outside posts, consistently spaced away from the inside posts, and anchor them with temporary braces. Attach strips of plywood to the posts on each side, level with each other. Because the plywood is only 8 feet (2.5m) long, you will need to use several pieces, with butt joints landing on the posts. Check that the plywood strips are level with each other as you attach them.

Use a level and framing square to mark and cut notches in the plywood so that you end up with stringers that are level with each other. Install three more layers of plywood, notched to match, for each stringer. Each piece will be slightly different from the underlying one, so hold them in place as you mark them.

Build a landing at the bottom of the stairway. Install the treads; the front tread is full width, and the back tread is rip-cut at an angle. Add fascia and other trim. Bend railing pieces, and install them as you did for the deck railing.

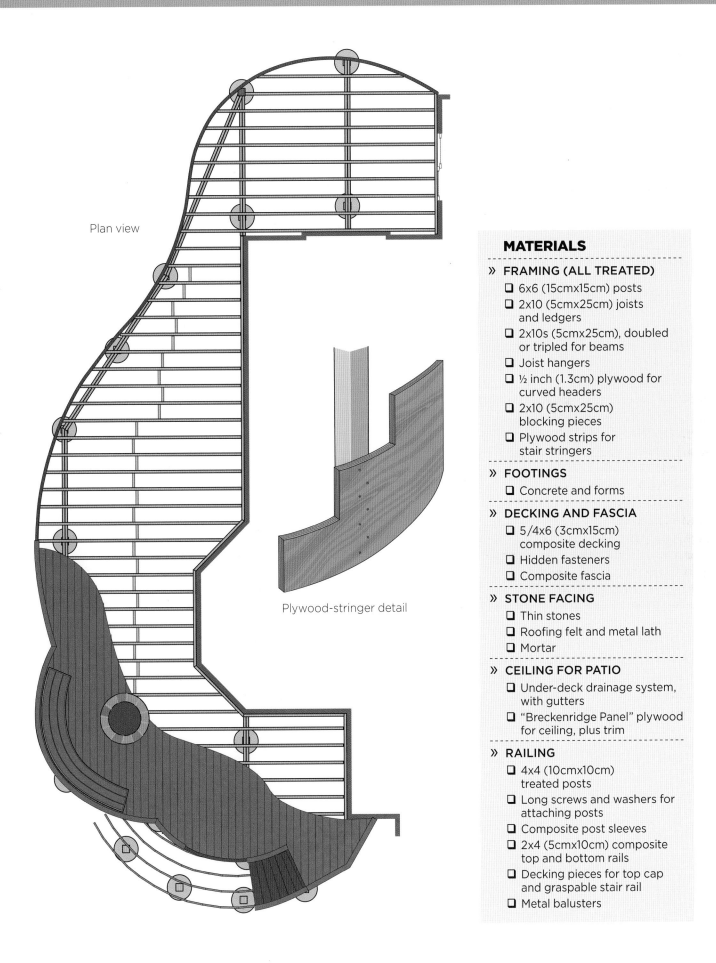

Plan view

Plywood-stringer detail

MATERIALS

» **FRAMING (ALL TREATED)**
- ❑ 6x6 (15cmx15cm) posts
- ❑ 2x10 (5cmx25cm) joists and ledgers
- ❑ 2x10s (5cmx25cm), doubled or tripled for beams
- ❑ Joist hangers
- ❑ ½ inch (1.3cm) plywood for curved headers
- ❑ 2x10 (5cmx25cm) blocking pieces
- ❑ Plywood strips for stair stringers

» **FOOTINGS**
- ❑ Concrete and forms

» **DECKING AND FASCIA**
- ❑ 5/4x6 (3cmx15cm) composite decking
- ❑ Hidden fasteners
- ❑ Composite fascia

» **STONE FACING**
- ❑ Thin stones
- ❑ Roofing felt and metal lath
- ❑ Mortar

» **CEILING FOR PATIO**
- ❑ Under-deck drainage system, with gutters
- ❑ "Breckenridge Panel" plywood for ceiling, plus trim

» **RAILING**
- ❑ 4x4 (10cmx10cm) treated posts
- ❑ Long screws and washers for attaching posts
- ❑ Composite post sleeves
- ❑ 2x4 (5cmx10cm) composite top and bottom rails
- ❑ Decking pieces for top cap and graspable stair rail
- ❑ Metal balusters

Private Family Room

Here is a space that feels shady, protected, and comfortable. Like a large fresh-air great room, this space serves several functions: it includes a spa, a luxury outdoor kitchen, and a cozy area for buffet dining and campfires. The curvy shape brightens the overall design and makes it a special place for family and small gatherings.

The Design

Though they had only a small space with which to work, the family wanted an outdoor kitchen with plenty of amenities, room for a fire pit and living room, and a roof to cover about two-thirds the deck, so they would be able to enjoy it when weather was bad. A spa was also on the wish list; a dining table was less important. Streett built a beautiful deck that suits their lifestyle to a T.

SIZE AND SHAPE. The space for the deck is a 27-foot-long (8.2m) alcove at the back of the house. The family did not want the deck to protrude outward too far into the yard, and Streett agreed; a larger deck would overpower the house and seem out of place.

Living room. An area about 300 square feet (27.9m²)—or just over 15 x 15 feet (4.6m x 4.6m)— is just right for a medium-size living room with fire pit.

Easy spa access. The spa rests on a concrete pad raised about 7½ inches (19.1cm). A variety of levels (from the stairs) for climbing in and out make access easy for all ages, and wide stairs also provide casual seating for those who prefer socializing to soaking.

Roof posts. Cedar posts, which support the roof, are joined to the glue-laminated beam with brackets. The bottom 4-foot (1.2m) section is clad with stone facing.

The deck design features his signature curves. On a deck this small there was no need to throw in an S-curve for visual interest. A single standard-radius bump-out, with straight lines on each side, looks complex enough. An added patio made of stamped and stained concrete offers its own curves and creates a fun transition to the yard.

Instead of a dining room there is a sort of all-purpose area that includes stuffed chairs, a fire pit, and occasional tables. Food can be brought directly from the indoor kitchen to this area, or it can be served buffet style in the outdoor kitchen on the other end.

Spas are often placed in a destination area well away from dining and cooking areas, but this deck design integrates it for a cozy effect. Placed just in front of the deck and unsheltered by a roof, spa bathers are safely out of range of grilling smoke and can enjoy the starlight once the sun goes down. Given the size of the deck, the spa feels remarkably like its own space.

The deck is about 28 inches (71cm) above grade—just under the 30-inch (76cm) height where a railing would be required by code. With no railing, the deck has an open, spacious feel.

Heating and cooling. The fan was installed well away from light fixtures; putting them too close can create an annoying strobe-light effect. Infrared heating units radiate a surprising amount of heat and make a room comfortable on cold days, unless there is a strong wind.

Coordinating patio. This stamped-concrete patio, with shades of blue and gray that resonate with the house color, makes a pleasant transition to the green lawn.

Kitchen amenities. The outdoor kitchen has plenty of bells and whistles, and it is open to the air on three sides while still being sheltered from above.

Rustic overhead. This charming ceiling, with its combination of skylights, sleek lighting, pine paneling, and natural pine glue-laminated beams, has a rustic, cottage-like ambiance.

Outdoor kitchen. The outdoor kitchen is on the far side of the deck from the kitchen door. Because of the overhead, it was necessary to put the grill on the periphery with open space on three sides so that cooking smoke can dissipate. (If a grill is placed near walls and is covered by a roof, you would need to install a commercial-grade exhaust fan, or diners would find themselves choking from the smoke.) A spacious traffic path makes the indoor kitchen easily accessible.

The outdoor kitchen counter is faced with thin stone and topped by a granite counter with colors to match the hues in the facing stones. It includes a large gas grill, a refrigerator, storage doors and drawers, and a double side-burner. (Like many builders in areas with freezing winters, Streett tries to talk homeowners out of a sink with running water because if they forget to shut off and drain the supply and drain lines prior to winter (easily done!), the pipes will freeze—with disastrous results.)

THE ROOF. A roof overhead was high on the list of priorities, but a number of builders had said it could not be done. Sometimes you have to keep looking for the right builder: Streett carefully installed a watertight roof that blends well with the house.

He built the roofline at an angle that fits naturally with the house's architecture—and with no visible sections of unsightly metal flashing. For the front roof beam, Streett used a glue-laminated lumber, which can span a long distance. That means that there is only one post near the middle of the span; a second post would have made the deck feel more constrained.

A pair of skylights brings in natural light while sealing out rain, and recessed canister lights brighten the space at night.

To make the deck usable most of the year, a ceiling fan provides a pleasant breeze during the summer, and electric infrared heating units keep things comfortable on frosty nights. These heating units are popular because they provide ample directed heat for a small energy cost. Homeowners claim that they extend the outdoor season by as much as two or three months.

Building the Deck

Because the spa will rest on concrete rather than framing, have the patio poured first; then build the deck. In this case, the concrete was formed and poured one stair-step higher, where the spa goes.

FRAMING. Use high-quality lumber for all of the framing. This deck is enclosed on three sides by the house and the steps, so there is little ventilation. That is not a problem in a dry climate like Colorado's, but in your area you may need to ventilate the underside of the deck using lattice sections.

Pour the concrete patio and the raised concrete section for the spa. Dig straight rows of postholes, and pour concrete footings according to local codes. Install the ledger against the house using code-approved fasteners and flashing.

Build the framing on temporary supports: most codes require joists to be installed 12 inches (30.5cm) apart where composite decking will run at an angle. Attach joists to the ledger using joist hangers, and let them run long. Install blocking, and check that the joists are correctly positioned at the ends away from the house. Use a chalk line to mark the tops of the joists for straight cuts on each side. Mark for the cuts with a square, and cut using a circular saw.

For the arced section, mark the tops of the joist for cutting using a string-and-pencil compass. Cut the joist ends, adjusting the circular saw's bevel slightly for each cut. Attach the two straight header joists; they can run a bit long on the inside of the deck. Make a header for the curved section using three layers of ½-inch (1.3cm) plywood strips. (See page 128 for more instructions.)

Run electrical and plumbing lines for the lights and spa.

STAIRS, DECKING, AND FASCIA. For the wide stairs you will need to cut quite a few 2x12 (5cmx30cm) stringers. Attach them to the header at the top and to the concrete at the bottom.

Install the decking using hidden fasteners. Cut decking ends at 45 degrees, and allow the pieces to overhang. Use a chalk line to mark the ends for straight cuts; use a string-and-pencil compass to mark for the curved cut. Make cuts using a circular saw. Cut and install fascia to cover the cut decking ends.

Use a deck oven or blanket heater to warm up decking pieces to be used as curved stair treads, and press them against jigs, as shown on pages 130–131. Install the fascia; then install the riser lights and then the treads.

OUTDOOR KITCHEN. Build the outdoor kitchen by framing it with metal or wood studs and cladding with concrete backer board. Have the appliances, doors, and drawers on hand to make sure your openings are correct. Run electrical lines, and install receptacles and lights. Cover the backer board with roofing felt, metal lath, and thin facing stones. Install the granite countertop, then the appliances and doors. (For full instructions, see Creative Homeowner's *Building Outdoor Kitchens for Every Budget*.)

THE ROOF. Only experienced roofers should tackle this job, but here is an overview: Attach the cedar roof posts to the decking using approved hardware. They should rest directly above a joist and a beam. Brace them temporarily in place, making sure they are plumb. Order glue-laminated beams to fit, and install them; where they meet the house you may support them with a post against the house or by cutting a pocket hole and inserting them. Install the rafters, and frame for the skylights. Run electrical lines, and install boxes for the lights and fan.

Cut away the house's siding where the roof will meet it. Cut and attach plywood sheathing, and add roofing felt. Install flashing at the top. Install the skylights, and flash them as needed. Install flashing at the outer edges of the roof, and apply shingles. At the sloped end where the roof meets the siding, install individual pieces of step flashing as you go, and tuck them under the siding pieces so they will not be visible.

Cover the underside of the rafters with tongue-and-groove siding. Make cutouts for the electrical boxes, and trim around the skylight. Add the light fixtures and trim, and install the fan.

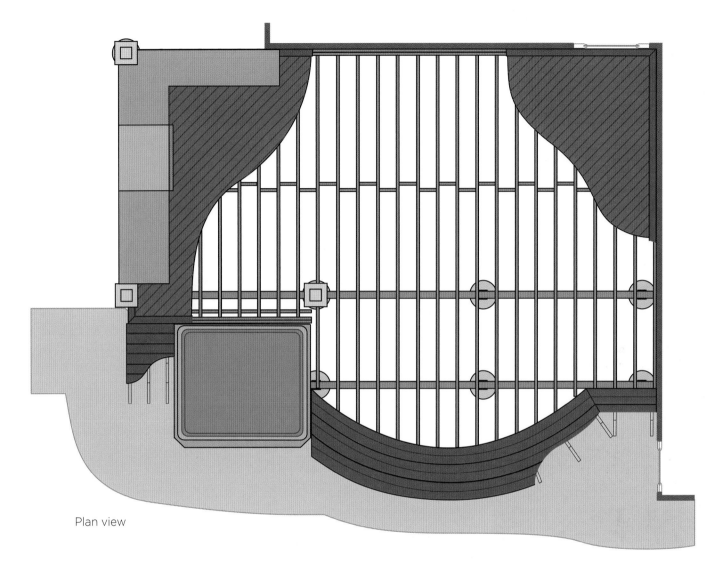

Plan view

MATERIALS

» **FRAMING (ALL TREATED)**
- ❑ 6x6 (15cmx15cm) posts
- ❑ 2x10 (5cmx25cm) joists, ledgers, and straight headers
- ❑ 2x10s (5cmx25cm), tripled for beams
- ❑ Joist hangers
- ❑ ½ inch (1.3cm) plywood for curved headers
- ❑ 2x10 (5cmx25cm) blocking pieces
- ❑ 2x12 (5cmx30cm) for stair stringers

» **FOOTINGS**
- ❑ Concrete and forms
- ❑ Hardware for posts and beams

» **DECKING AND FASCIA**
- ❑ 5/4x6 (3cmx15cm) composite decking
- ❑ Hidden fasteners
- ❑ Composite fascia

» **STONE FACING**
- ❑ Thin stones
- ❑ Roofing felt and metal lath
- ❑ Mortar

» **ROOF**
- ❑ Glue-laminated beams
- ❑ 6x6 (15cmx15cm) cedar posts
- ❑ 2x10 (5cmx25cm) rafters
- ❑ Skylights
- ❑ Lights, fan, and wiring
- ❑ Plywood sheathing
- ❑ Roofing felt, shingles, and flashing
- ❑ Tongue-and-groove siding for the ceiling

Rocky Mountain High Life

Because of the steep slope at the back of the house, this high-end deck takes the place of a backyard. Stone and wood-toned composite surfaces make it feel right at home in its rocky forest setting.

The Design

The customers wanted a large, interesting-looking space to emphasize the treetop view. Their backyard is flat for 4 to 5 feet (1.2m to 1.5m) near the house, then drops off steeply. There is a lovely view of the Colorado Rockies out the back of the house on the second floor; building a deck that extends out at that level makes it even better.

SHAPES AND SIZES. A major theme here is simply "big." In each of its use areas, the deck is a large blank canvas where people can relax and enjoy a feeling of space and openness. Walkways are wider than they need to be, and seating areas have extra room.

As with most of Streett's decks, there are plenty of curves. The upper level offers two sections defined by outward curves; the inward curve in the middle coincides with a bump-out at the house to clearly mark the areas as

separate. As you leave the house, a dining area is to the left, and the outdoor kitchen is to the right. So both spaces have easy access to the indoor kitchen and to each other, yet cooking smoke blows away. (The upper level is mostly covered by a third-level deck, which we will not discuss here.)

If you walk from the outdoor kitchen to the lowest level, you pass through a series of cascading landings; walking directly from the house kitchen, you reach the lower level via wide, arcing steps.

The lower level features a large outcropping deck area that juts heroically into the landscape. Even though it drops four steps down from the upper level at its most forward point, this area sits about 18 feet (5.5m) above grade. It captures a panoramic view of surrounding scenery, including a nearby manmade waterfall.

Stone facing. Chopped thin-stone facing must be installed with tight joints. This planter has a galvanized lining, so there is no worry about rust.

Unique bench. The curved bench, capped and faced with stones, offers partially reclined seating oriented toward the great view.

Kitchen convenience. The outdoor kitchen features a capacious grill, storage, and a refrigerator, as well as a combination sink and ice cooler to keep sodas and brews icy and easy to grab.

Gathering space. The overhang on the kitchen counter provides plenty of room for eating and drinking and to "belly up to the bar."

BENCH, PLANTERS, AND RAILING. An unusual curved bench, located in the middle of the deck on the house side, provides couch-like seating. The back and seat are made of decking with capstones topping off the bench and thin stones providing stylish cover for the area under the seating. Built-in planters covered with the same thin stones flank the bench on each side.

Several large wooden planters covered with thin stones help tie the design together while adding splashes of color. The planters are made of treated plywood and have galvanized liners, which prevent rust and lengthen the life of the wood.

The railing, made of natural cedar with a dark stain, follows the curved and straight lines of the deck. Massive 6x6 (15cmx15cm) posts suit the character of the spacious setting, and thin, dark metal balusters barely inhibit the view.

BAR-STYLE OUTDOOR KITCHEN. This outdoor kitchen is not very close to the indoor kitchen, which is the usual arrangement, and has enough amenities to function on its own. The large gas grill can handle just about any barbecue challenge. Most of the time, however, the homeowners use the kitchen like a bar in a finished basement. For that reason, it has a sink with running water, an ice-filled cooler, a refrigerator, and an overhanging counter where you can pull up bar stools.

MATERIALS. The decking is a composite material that looks and feels a lot like natural wood. This is partly because it has a matte rather than shiny finish and partly because there is greater-than-usual variation in color and pattern. Materials like this cost more but make a deck feel more natural while retaining the low-maintenance advantage of composites. The decking runs in several directions, helping to define various areas.

The thin stone used for the outdoor kitchen, planters, and bench siding is "chopped," meaning it is hand cut. It is installed dry stacked, without mortar in the joints. This is a more challenging installation because the pieces have to fit together tightly, but the results look more like solid stone.

Dark accents. The railing is made of cedar, stained dark. Under the deck is a private place for a hammock with a close-up view of the waterfall.

Peaceful getaway. The deck steps down into a natural, restful hideaway, complete with a water feature.

Lighting options. Pendant lights over the counter dangle from the handsome ceiling paneled with stained tongue-and-groove planks.

179

Building the Deck

A massive elevated structure like this is a major undertaking, calling for the expertise of experienced professionals. Because of the height, extra-large posts are required. Choose massive lumber pieces carefully. They should be rated No. 1 or select and kiln dried, so they will not warp or crack.

FRAMING. The framing is complicated because different levels share beams. Make sure various levels are multiples of 7½ inches (19.1cm) higher or lower than each other. Install the ledger; then build the joist sections on temporary supports. Install curved headers where needed. (See page 128.) Build and attach beams to the undersides of the joists. Dig postholes, pour footings according to code, and install posts to support the beams.

RAILING AND DECKING. Install the railing posts inside the framing, and attach blocking to keep the posts firm. Run wiring for the riser lights.

Install decking at various angles, using hidden fasteners. Cut the decking flush to the headers and outside joists, and install fascia that covers the cut ends of decking pieces.

Build railing sections that fit between the posts. Build the straight sections using 2x4 (5cmx10cm) top and bottom rails with evenly spaced balusters. Attach the sections, and add 1x4 (2.5cmx10cm) pieces on the sides of the posts. Make curved sections using 2x10s (5cmx25cm) or 2x12s (5cmx30cm), as needed. Cut them so that they follow the deck's curve and are 3½ inches (8.9cm) wide.

BENCH AND PLANTER. Build the bench using 2x4s (5cmx10cm) and 2x12s (5cmx30cm) for framing, as shown in the illustration on page 181. Cover the front and top with treated ½-inch (1.3cm) plywood, and install stone facing and cap pieces. Use a heating pad or oven to bend the decking pieces for the seat.

Make planters out of simple 2x4 (5cmx10cm) frames and treated plywood sheathing. Cover the plywood with thin stone, and hire a fabricator to make galvanized linings to fit. Set the liners in, and add capstones.

MATERIALS

» **FRAMING (ALL TREATED)**
- ❑ 6x6 (15cmx15cm) and 8x8 (20cmx20cm) posts
- ❑ 2x10 (5cmx25cm) and 2x8 (5cmx20cm) joists, ledgers, and straight headers
- ❑ 2x10s (5cmx25cm), tripled or doubled for beams
- ❑ Joist hangers
- ❑ ½ inch (1.3cm) plywood for curved headers
- ❑ 2x10 (5cmx25cm) blocking pieces
- ❑ 2x12s (5cmx30cm) for stair stringers

» **FOOTINGS**
- ❑ Concrete and forms
- ❑ Hardware for posts and beams

» **DECKING AND FASCIA**
- ❑ 5/4x6 (3cmx15cm) composite decking
- ❑ Hidden fasteners
- ❑ Composite fascia

» **BENCHES AND PLANTERS**
- ❑ Treated 2x4s (5cmx10cm) and 2x12s (5cmx30cm) for framing
- ❑ Treated ½ inch (1.3cm) plywood
- ❑ Roofing felt, metal lath, and mortar
- ❑ Thin facing stones
- ❑ Galvanized planter liners

» **RAILING (ALL CEDAR)**
- ❑ 6x6 (15cmx15cm) posts
- ❑ 2x4s (5cmx10cm) or 2x10s (5cmx25cm) for top and bottom rails
- ❑ 2x4s (5cmx10cm), 2x10s (5cmx25cm), or 2x12s (5cmx30cm) for top caps
- ❑ 1x4 (2.5cmx10cm) trim on side of posts
- ❑ Metal balusters

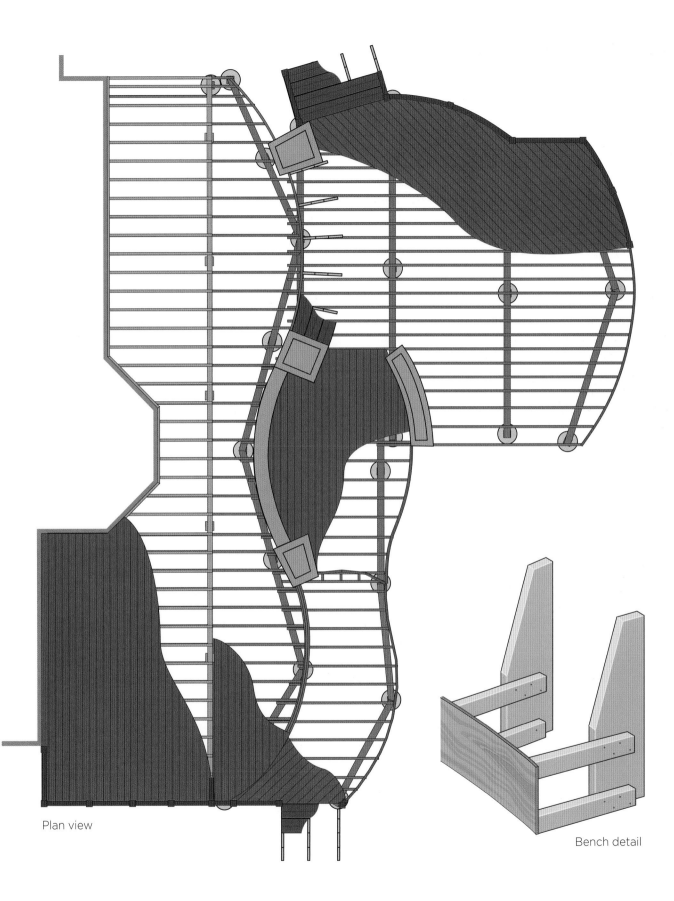

Plan view

Bench detail

Clough Construction

Scott and Deanne Clough have run Clough Construction, a family business in Marin County, California, for more than twenty-six years. In that time, they have established a solid reputation as builders of top-quality decks. They usually keep five crews with as many as seventeen workers busy.

Marin County has many large homes overlooking spectacular views, but there are also friendly neighborhood areas with less-expensive homes. As you might imagine, decks range widely in size and price.

Interesting shapes. Wide stairs are always an inviting hangout spot. Here, a row of trapezoidal platforms on the side of the house make a nice transition to the outdoors, where the setting sun makes the distant landscape glow.

Scott and Deanne Clough

CLOUGH CONSTRUCTION

San Rafael, California
415-444-5554
www. cloughconstruction. com

DESIGN APPROACHES

Marin County is hilly almost everywhere, so outdoor living space is often at a premium. A deck may become a family's backyard and its main outdoor living center. People with small boxy decks tacked onto the back of their houses are often frustrated: they can look outside and see great views, but they cannot live and relax there. Building beautiful decks with functional, well-sized "outdoor rooms" can, in the Cloughs' experience, transform people's lives. Typically, customers say, they spend much more time outside enjoying their new fresh-air living space.

The Cloughs see a deck as a bridge between the home and the natural world. Though their decks often end up raised 8 feet (2.5m) or more above grade, they take every opportunity to create graceful walkways and transitions to the yard. This may mean a series of cascading levels or a stepped walkway (rather than a simple stairway) leading from the yard to the deck.

Large outdoor kitchens are not usually part of their projects because their customers tend to want to use the deck space for hanging out—lounging, conversing, and enjoying the fresh air. When they do cook outside, it tends to be a more modest endeavor. Many Clough decks serve as play centers for families with young children or places to roughhouse with the dog. Some include sandboxes or even basketball hoops.

MATERIALS. Although the Cloughs occasionally build with composite materials, the majority of their clients prefer natural wood. The most common choice is redwood, a traditional California building material that makes a beautiful transition between a man-made structure and a wooded property. Many of their clients feel that having natural materials is well worth the extra maintenance.

Not all customers want wood decks, however; composites *are* growing in popularity in California, though not as fast as in other parts of the country. The Cloughs have been building composite decks for more than ten years, and in that time they have come across composites that do not wear well. Some manufacturers have made changes that have greatly improved quality, though, so knowing this, the Cloughs can offer their customers the best composite products at reasonable prices.

Personal embellishments. A solid fence-like redwood railing with a wide top cap is a pleasant perch for an iconic relief sculpture.

Lots of space. In an inviting tree-house-like setting, this activity center for the homeowners' children has plenty of room for small wheeled vehicles and a large gravel-and-sand play area.

Spectacular setting. Views in Marin County can be stunning. Here the view from the spa and its adjacent deck features the area's distinctive rolling fog washing over the landscape.

Elegant design. A simple yet elegant complexity makes this section of one of the Cloughs' decks special. Angles, curves, and variations in levels work together to create a space that seems to gracefully roll with the natural setting.

Kids' space. A second children's play area, built in a cozy niche beneath the branches of a favorite tree, offers a place for private play with benches for grownup visitors.

SUSTAINABILITY. Many years ago, the Cloughs' daughter asked Scott if he was worried about all of the redwood trees that were being cut down to make decks. This planted an acorn of an idea. They had become acutely aware of how many building processes—including or maybe especially decks—consume natural resources that are not easily renewable. As a result, they felt that they should reorient their business toward eco-friendly approaches and the use of sustainable lumber.

Nowadays the Cloughs seek to use materials that support long-term ecological balance. The materials are organic, locally grown, and responsibly harvested so that they do not deplete natural resources. Using composite lumber is another approach.

To produce green-friendly decks using redwood, they buy their lumber from Humboldt Redwood Company, based in California. Many people are surprised to learn that building with redwood can be eco-friendly. The Forest Stewardship Council (FSC) certifies Humboldt lumber, meaning that Humboldt harvests it in a renewable way. (For more information on sustainable redwood, see pages 196–197.) Typically, FSC-certified lumber costs about 10 percent more than standard lumber—a small price to pay for sustainability, the Cloughs feel.

ENGINEERING FOR STRENGTH

Because of the high slopes in their area, the Cloughs' decks must be carefully engineered. Codes in Marin County are strict and specific, so a structural engineer must verify plans. It can often take four to six months for a plan to be approved, and a permit can cost thousands of dollars.

On large decks the foundation can be as substantial as that of a house. The Cloughs often use extra-large beams and posts, sometimes with extensive cross-bracing. The goal is not just to meet code but also to produce a deck with no squeaks or bounce, a deck that will remain stable for many decades.

Unique finishes. This small balcony deck has an unusual ceramic tile floor, wood railing, and a painted top cap.

Excellent carpentry. Carefully crafted joints like these call for great carpentry skills and great lumber.

Wood cabinets. This outdoor kitchen, made of hardwood cabinets and a tiled countertop, takes advantage of the shade from a nearby tree.

Design details. The basket-weave-like pattern in this railing, made with redwood 2x2s (5cmx5cm), provides a stylish frame for the view.

Spa space. Meandering railroad-tie steps lead to a private platform deck with spa.

Strong structure. Beautiful decks are often supported by very business-like concrete footings, hardware, posts, and cross braces.

Clean design. The simple lines of this low deck with gently cascading steps contribute to a Zen-like atmosphere.

Clough Techniques

1 The Cloughs consult with engineers and get engineering approval for plans to make sure that their decks will be strong and durable.

2 Footings are often massive and sunk very deep to carry extra-heavy loads. The footings are generally steel-reinforced for extra stability.

3 Even when codes do not require it, the Cloughs usually install joists on 12-inch (30.5cm) centers. Again, this adds rigidity and strength.

4 Scott anchors ledgers using special hardware that goes into the house. The hardware ensures not only that the ledger will stay attached but also that the joists will not come loose from the ledger.

5 The FSA-approved redwood that the Cloughs so often use is not just eco-friendly but also exceptionally stable. Decks that are ten years and older typically show almost no cracking, checking, or warping.

Intricate angles. The neat geometric confluence of angles of the decking boards on stairways and walkways has a logic that neatly fits within the natural setting.

Natural Jewel

With all visible surfaces—decking, railings, stairs—made of redwood, this multilevel backyard platform seems connected to its setting. The design is pleasantly simple, dressed up with a few details. A tree growing through the deck increases the natural appeal.

The Design

The goals here were modest. In a small yard space, the owners wanted a place for intimate dining, relaxing on lounge chairs, and some potted plants. They chose to integrate a lovely tree growing on the site rather than cut it down. The deck is oriented toward a magnificent view.

SHAPE AND SIZE. From the kitchen door you walk onto a landing about 6 x 10 feet (1.8m x 3m). The landing has its own railing, though it is not required by code: the railing provides a place to lean out and enjoy the view from the deck's highest point, and it adds a measure of complexity to the overall design.

The main deck is two steps down from the landing, which is also reachable from sliding doors off the living room. The area next to the landing has a tree growing through it, a perfect shady spot for a pair of lounge chairs. A small dining table fits near the perimeter railing, leaving plenty of open space for potted plants and a small water feature.

A 3-foot-wide (91cm) stairway in one direction leads to the yard, which makes for easy traffic flow from the kitchen to the backyard. In the other direction, a small 6-foot-wide (1.8m) deck, two steps down from the main deck, serves as a spacious walkway from a bedroom door to the main deck; it is just wide enough to accommodate either a couple of chairs with an end table or more plants.

Amazing view. The view cascades down toward the horizon in the distance, and the built-in tree blurs the distinction between the deck and the wide, wide world.

Expert craftsmanship. This mitered corner of the rail cap is remarkably tight and warp-free; on lesser decks this is a point where lumber and joinery may fail after a couple of years or so.

Inexpensive additions. A water feature like this, with a spouting frog, is inexpensive and easy to install. It makes a gentle gurgling sound and can be wired to make it easy to turn on and off.

Carpentry skill. Places like this, where the stair rail meets the deck rail, showcase the skill of experienced carpenters. The clean-looking graspable handrail is made of neatly cut, rounded, and assembled 2x2s (5cmx5cm).

Finishing details. Railing fastener heads are mostly hidden, except for a few that are unavoidably visible. The angled scarf joint on top of the post has a more finished appearance than a straight butt joint would. Wiring for the light discreetly runs through a groove in the back of the post, which is then covered by trim.

MATERIALS. The Cloughs built the deck using FSC redwood, an important consideration to the clients, who want to be gentle on the environment. The deck is more than 6 years old, but the decking and railings remain free of cracks and warps, and the joints are still tight. Only high-quality, stable wood that is dry when purchased can perform like that. With lesser quality lumber, gaps at the corners of the rail cap and in the end joints on the decking would surely open up; the boards would become wavy; and cracks would develop.

The decking and the rail cap are made of clear wood, meaning that it has no knots. The riser and fascia boards have some tight knots, which adds appealing texture to the look. In a sunny place like this, redwood should be sealed with a semitransparent stain at least once a year.

TREE HOLE. The tree is a slow-growing oak. The deck was built around it with about 6 inches (15.2cm) of space between framing members (the joists and blocking). Decking boards were cut to fit with a 1½-inch (4cm) space all around. As the tree grows, the decking can be recut using a jigsaw to accommodate the greater girth.

RAILING. The railing design most often used by the Cloughs is all redwood, with no metal balusters or hardware, built so there will be few visible screw heads—only at places like mitered corners on the top cap. They attach posts to the outside of joists and headers, afterward adding fascia between the posts so that the posts look as if they are notched in.

Incorporating natural elements.
Though it involves extra work (and expense), incorporating a tree in the design generally improves the overall look and functioning of a deck. Here it provides welcome shade and a natural connection to the landscape beyond.

Personal embellishments. A corner nook is the perfect spot for personal touches—here, a grouping of plants and a statue adds a dash of Zen.

Straightforward design. A simple stairway leads to the backyard.

Furniture selection.
For a small deck, a clear round glass table is a great choice; it has a more open feel, so you can see more of the deck, and it is easy to add one more chair to a circle when needed.

Building the Deck

Here the Cloughs placed a beam near the house for support in addition to the ledger. Your codes may not require this beam.

FRAMING. Install the ledgers using strong fasteners and flashing that will keep the house and framing dry. Ledgers for different levels should be multiples of 7½ inches (19.1cm) higher or lower than each other, for steps with consistent heights.

Build the framing on temporary supports. Attach joists to the ledger using joist hangers, and allow them to run long past the temporary supports. Install rows of blocking as needed. Around the tree, cut joists and install blocking as needed to keep all framing boards at least 6 inches (15.2cm) away from the tree.

Attach the beams to the undersides of the joists using temporary supports, and dig straight rows of postholes under them. Pour concrete footings to meet local codes. Install the support posts between the footings and the beams, using hardware for the attachments.

Make sure that all of the joists are correctly spaced at the ends. Mark their tops for straight cuts using a chalk line; then draw square cut lines on each, and cut them using a circular saw. Fasten the header joist to the cut joist ends. Double the header and the outside joists. Install blocking where the railing posts will go so that the header or outside joist will be solid and will not wobble.

DECKING, RAILING, AND FASCIA. Install decking with ⅛-inch (0.3cm) gaps between the boards; use deck spacers or nails to make gaps. Install the first pieces flush with the outside of the header joists, using a string line to keep them straight. As you install the other pieces, check every third or fourth board for straightness, and make sure that the boards are parallel with the house; make slight adjustments if needed.

Attach the railing posts to the outside of the headers' end joists using lag screws or bolts. Cut and install the fascia boards so that they come flush with the decking surface and span between the railing posts.

Build baluster sections with evenly spaced balusters to fit between posts, as shown in the illustration on page 195. Attach the sections to the sides of the posts 4 inches (10cm) below the post tops using angle-driven screws. Install a 2x6 (5cmx15cm) cap on top of the posts; miter the corners. At the stair railing, build a handrail on one side using rounded 2x2s (5cmx5cm) and long screws.

MATERIALS

» **FRAMING (ALL TREATED)**
- ❑ 4x4 (10cmx10cm) posts
- ❑ 2x8 (5cmx20cm) joists, ledgers, and headers
- ❑ 4x8 (10cmx20cm) beams
- ❑ Joist hangers
- ❑ 2x10 (5cmx25cm) blocking pieces
- ❑ 2x12s (5cmx30cm) for stair stringers

» **FOOTINGS**
- ❑ Concrete and forms
- ❑ Hardware for posts and beams

» **DECKING AND FASCIA**
- ❑ 2x6 (5cmx15cm) FSC redwood
- ❑ Stainless-steel screws
- ❑ 1-by (2.5cm-by) redwood for fascia

» **RAILING (ALL REDWOOD)**
- ❑ 4x4 (10cmx10cm) posts
- ❑ 2x4 (5cmx10cm) top and bottom rails
- ❑ 2x2s (5cmx5cm) for balusters and rails
- ❑ 2x6s (5cmx15cm) for the top cap

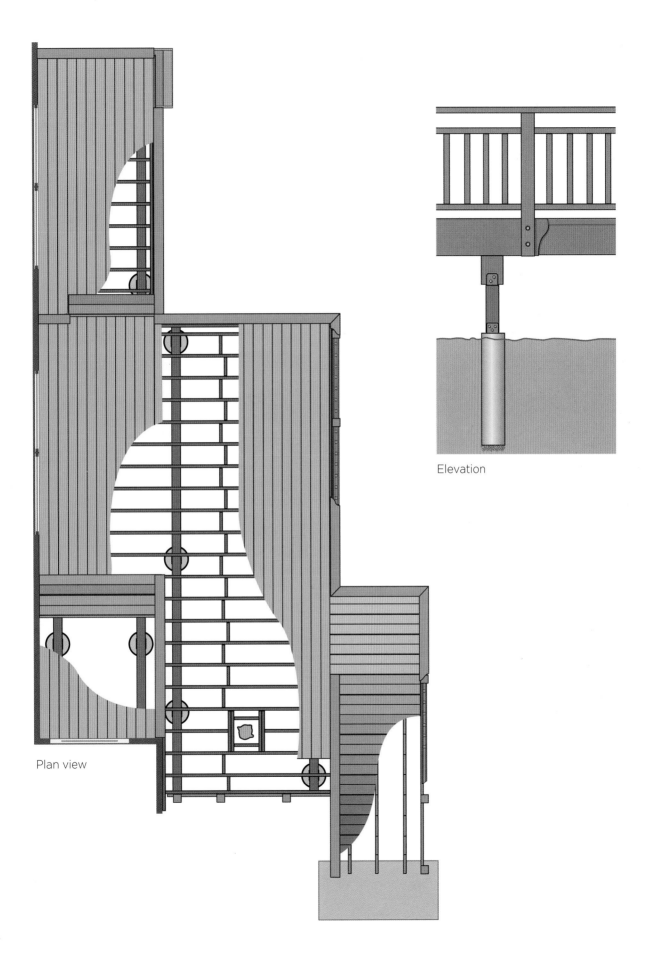

Elevation

Plan view

Earth-Friendly, Durable Redwood

Many people view redwood as an old-fashioned deck product, as well as a resource that is nearly depleted. But firms like the Humboldt Redwood Company have developed sustainable techniques for growing redwood so that harvested trees are replaced by new growth. The Forest Stewardship Council (FSC) has certified the trees as a renewable resource.

Humboldt owns a large tract of old-growth forest near Eureka, California, which they manage by pruning and select-cutting rather than clear-cutting. When the company's lumberjacks harvest a tree, they plant a new one in its place. In fact, they actually grow more than they harvest.

Redwood trees have a positive impact on Earth because they store rather than emit carbon more efficiently than other trees. Redwood is the fastest growing softwood species in North America, making it an efficient scrubber of greenhouse gases. The faster trees grow, the more carbon they absorb. Younger trees grow fast, but older trees grow slowly and decay—they may actually release more carbon than they absorb. So managed harvesting of older trees may actually be in the interest of the planet. Another consideration: In 50 to 100 years, if a redwood structure needs to be demolished, it will go back to the earth gracefully.

This is not "farmed" lumber that is designed to grow quickly. Boards from farmed trees tend to have wide growth rings, making them weaker and vulnerable to cracking and warping. Instead, FSC lumber has narrow, straight grain, which means that the boards will stay straight and true for a long time. By select-cutting, Humboldt maintains a natural forest with variously sized trees—many of them quite large—rather than the little same-size trees that grow after clear-cutting.

Last points: redwood has a low thermal conductivity, meaning that it will not overheat on summer days. It also has a Class B fire rating and is approved in many areas where wildfires are a danger.

Lightly stained, high-quality redwood can feature mellow tones like taupe.

Redwood with large knots creates a beautifully pied appearance. Be sure that the knots are tight, and keep them well sealed so that they don't come loose.

A tree pokes exuberantly up through a hole in the deck, and looks especially at home because the decking is natural redwood. The framing that supports the decking makes an opening about 16 inches larger in diameter than the tree, so the decking can be periodically cut with a jigsaw as the tree grows in girth.

Occasional additions of color, like the blue top rail of this railing, lend a playful touch and help clearly define shapes. In the case of a top rail, which often gets handled, there is a practical side as well: a well-painted surface is easier to wipe clean than finished wood. The post top is given a simple but classic treatment, produced by bevel-cutting each side. The resulting shape effectively sheds rainwater, thereby preventing wet rot.

Kept well protected by regular applications of sealer, redwood makes a stunning poolside surface. Here the perimeter of the pool is decked with natural stone, which may be installed following methods like those shown on pages 210–211.

The Cloughs' decks often orient carefully toward the view. Here the upper deck features a railing with a wide top cap, perfect for leaning against while taking in the vistas and the meandering foggy wisps so common in the Bay area. The lower level houses a spa that is raised enough so soaking folks gain a clear view above the railing.

Sunset Setting

With its redwood overhead and railing, this deck feels a bit like a mountain cabin. But composite decking gives it the modern convenience of easy maintenance. Along the way, it achieves the perfect combination of light and shade.

The Design

This deck started with a major design challenge: A new public-easement walkway runs at an angle next to the house and is quite close to the front of the house. That made the existing rectangular deck obsolete: it was now out of compliance and illegal. A new deck had to be built at a different angle.

SIZE AND SHAPE. The angled side of the deck is as wide as the law will permit, where it follows along the public easement line. Walking out the side door (the only access to the deck), you enter a walkway that starts out only 4 feet (1.2m) wide, then widens as you walk toward the deck. A stairway near the door has a gate at the top to keep the dog in.

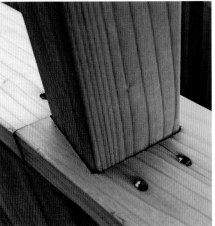

Pet-friendly materials. The canine resident is large and active, but the top-quality decking shows nary a mark from his claws.

Unique construction. The overhead support posts face forward, while the deck is at an angle, leading to this unusual conjunction.

Natural light. The changing position of the sun as it sets can dramatically alter the shadows cast during the course of supper.

Overhead. The overhead is a complex geometric combination of 2x8 (5cmx 20cm), 2x6 (5cmx15cm), 2x4 (5cmx 10cm), and 2x2 (5cmx5cm) boards.

The main deck is 17 x 12 feet (5.2m x 3.7m), a modest size, but the family reports it is plenty of room for a convivial evening outdoors. The living room area has lots of comfortable seating and a fire pit that doubles as a coffee table.

RAILING. On one side there is a standard open railing with balusters spaced 4 inches (10cm) apart. On the other, angled side, the homeowners chose to install a solid railing, like a fence. The railing provides privacy by blocking the view from the nearby public walkway but also allows the owners to enjoy the scenic vista in the distance.

OVERHEAD. The deck has a hot southwest exposure, so a shade structure was a must. The Cloughs spaced crisscrossing overhead pieces to provide partial shade as the sun moves across the sky. The varying width and spacing of boards casts shadows to ease the heat but admit enough light so that the deck still feels light and open.

Spacing overhead boards to achieve the right amount of shade is not a science but does require time and attention. Scott went to the deck on sunny days, at various times of day, to see which arrangements worked best. When the sun starts to sink in the west, the overhead makes dramatic shadows that both cool the space and soften the incoming light.

MATERIALS. The solid railing is made of FSC-approved Construction Heart redwood with rough-sawn knotty redwood that feels a bit like knotty interior paneling but with a slightly darker stain. The overhead is made of the same kind of lumber.

The decking is a super-durable composite, chosen in part because the large family dog is active and playful. Here, he can scamper and jump for hours without leaving a discernible scratch.

Solid railing. An attractive solid railing at just the right height provides welcome privacy while preserving a pleasant view.

Heavy-duty support. Building on a severe slope calls for extra-large concrete footings, heavy-duty cross braces, and serious fastening hardware.

Building the Deck

Building a deck on a steep slope calls for experienced workers, good scaffolding, and plenty of help. Erecting temporary supports for building the tallest point of the deck would take almost as much work as building the actual beam, so the Cloughs installed the footings, support posts, and beams first. They had their plans approved by an engineer, a must in such a challenging building environment.

FRAMING. Attach the ledger, 2½ inches (6.5cm) below the threshold, using strong fasteners and code-approved flashing. To locate the row of postholes on the steep slope, measure outward using a straight board with a level on top; then use a plumb bob to mark the hole locations. Dig the postholes, and pour the footings according to code. In this case, massive 16-inch-diameter (406. cm) footings were required.

Mount the support posts, longer than they need to be, onto the footings using approved hardware. Temporarily but firmly brace them so that they will stay level while you work; use 2x6 (5cmx15cm) braces and heavy-duty stakes. Use a level atop a board or a laser level to mark the posts for cutting, one beam's width below the bottom of the ledger. Cut the port using a circular saw, then a reciprocating saw. Attach the beam on top, using the correct hardware. Install the other two beams with posts and footings; allow them to run long for cutting later.

Install the joists, attaching them to the ledger at one end and allowing them to run long. Where there is no ledger, install them with blocking to keep them straight and firm, and attach them to the beams. Allow them to run long.

Mark the tops of the joists for cutting using a chalk line. Cut the joists using a circular saw; on the angled side, you will need to cut the steep angles using a reciprocating saw. Cut and install the header and the angled outside joist; then double them. Cut off the beams where they run long. Install a row of blocking for extra strength.

DECKING. Starting with the board that runs alongside the house, install the decking using a spacer between boards and stainless-steel screws. Check every few boards to see that they are straight. Allow the decking to run long; then make a chalk-line cut so that they end up flush with the outside of the headers and outside joists.

RAILINGS AND OVERHEAD. Install the railing posts using strong bolts or screws. Some of the posts double as overhead supports; install them at the correct height. To make the open railing, build 2x2 (5cmx5cm) sections with a 2x4 (5cmx10cm) at the bottom. Make the sections to fit between the posts, much as shown on page 195. Add a 2x6 (5cmx15cm) post cap; at the overhead posts, you will need to cut around them.

Install fascia boards on the outside joists and header, between the posts. Make their top edges flush with the decking surface.

For the solid railing, build fence sections to fit between the posts. Cut four 1x4s (2.5cmx10cm) to fit, and cut the 1x8s (2.5cmx20cm) to the desired height. Sandwich the vertical 1x8s (2.5cmx20cm) between the 1x4s (2.5cmx10cm) at top and bottom, and attach them by angle-driving screws into the posts. Add a 2x6 (5cmx15cm) top cap.

Make the overhead beams by attaching 2x8s (5cmx20cm) on each side of the tall posts; their tops should be flush with the tops of the posts. Attach evenly spaced 2x6 (5cmx15cm) rafters, then 2x4 (5cmx10cm) cross pieces. Top with evenly spaced 2x2s (5cmx5cm).

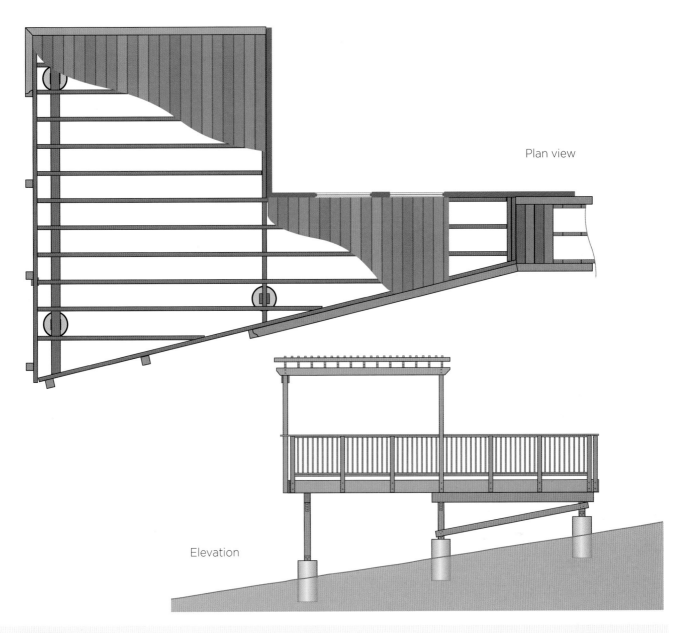

Plan view

Elevation

MATERIALS

» **FRAMING (ALL TREATED)**
- ❏ 6x6 (15cmx15cm) posts
- ❏ 2x6 (5cmx15cm) cross braces
- ❏ 2x10 (5cmx25cm) joists, ledgers, and headers
- ❏ 6x10 (15cmx25cm) beams
- ❏ Joist hangers
- ❏ 2x10 (5cmx25cm) blocking pieces
- ❏ 2x12s (5cmx30cm) for stair stringers

» **FOOTINGS**
- ❏ Concrete and forms
- ❏ Hardware for posts and beams

» **DECKING AND FASCIA**
- ❏ 2x6 (5cmx15cm) FSC redwood
- ❏ Stainless-steel screws
- ❏ 1-by (2.5cm-by) redwood for fascia

» **RAILING (ALL REDWOOD)**
- ❏ 4x4 (10cmx10cm) posts
- ❏ 2x4 (5cmx10cm) top and bottom rails
- ❏ 2x2s (5cmx5cm) for balusters and handrails
- ❏ 2x6 (5cmx15cm) top cap

» **SOLID RAILING**
- ❏ 1x4 (2.5cmx10cm) rough-sawn redwood for rails
- ❏ 1x8 (2.5cmx20cm) rough-sawn redwood for fencing
- ❏ 2x6 (5cmx15cm) smooth redwood for the top cap

» **OVERHEAD (ALL ROUGH-SAWN REDWOOD)**
- ❏ 2x8s (5cmx20cm) for beams
- ❏ 2x6 (5cmx15cm) rafters
- ❏ 2x4 (5cmx10cm) cross pieces
- ❏ 2x2 (5cmx5cm) top pieces

Movie Star Setting

By an existing swimming pool, wood or composite decking would be fine, but stone tiles provide the solid feel the owners were after. Fortunately, new products make it possible to install real tiles on top of wood framing.

The Design

The existing wood deck was water-damaged, and the owners just wanted a different surface—something more luxurious feeling and easier to keep clean than wood. The Cloughs told them about new stone tiles that they had come across, and the owners went for the idea.

The swimming pool was already solidly in place, and the framing was in good shape, so the main project was installing the tiles. Making this change completely transformed the appearance.

Relaxing space. The pool-house section feels like a cozy cabana getaway, complete with lounge chairs and casual tables.

Soft curves. Curves help soften the overall rectangular look of the deck; here, a curve by the entry landing seems appropriate beneath the home's curved second-floor balcony.

Private space. Behind the retaining wall, a few rustic steps form a path to a modest contemplative space.

THE LAYOUT. The Cloughs added another flourish: a curved bump-out dining area that protrudes toward the magnificent view. Though the radius of the arc is smaller it echoes curves in the house exterior—on the nearby balcony and the landing by the door—which helps unify the overall design.

There is a retaining wall along one side of the deck, holding back a hillside; a white lattice trellis fence covers part of the retaining wall. All around the deck, white-painted redwood trim ties in with the house trim. The Cloughs finished the edges, capped the top with white trim, and used wide boards to provide seating in some sections.

They also added a small pool house with an attached overhead structure. It is actually a small storeroom, but it adds to the feeling of luxury.

MATERIALS. The owners chose white-painted wood for the railing, overhead, benches, and lattice. These elements will need to be repainted every five or six years, but they preferred the more old-fashioned look and feel of painted wood over composite or vinyl.

The tiles are actually natural stone with a plastic backing that allows them to be installed onto wood.

Lattice and overhead. At the outside entrance, the overhead and lattice railing combine for an arbor effect.

Dining area. Now this is what you call dining al fresco—the quintessential outdoor room with a view.

Easy maintenance. The wood railing is expertly coated with glossy paint, so it is nearly as easy to clean as composite yet retains the charm of natural wood grain.

Slate decking. The slate deck surface has an overall blue-gray appearance; minor tones like rust or even purple add depth and appeal.

Material selection. White painted railings and natural stone tiles in varied slate tones are a handsome, formal combination that looks bright and inviting against the scenic backdrop.

Extreme structural support. An elevated swimming pool calls for huge reinforced-concrete posts and beams.

Detailed engineering. The curved, bumped-out dining area, erected high in the sky, needs massive timbers to support it. Structures like this require the design expertise of a structural engineer.

Building the Deck

Framing here is much like that on other decks. But the joists need to be exactly 16 inches (40.6cm) on center, that is, 16 inches (40.6cm) from the center of one joist's thickness to the center of the next joist's thickness. If the spacing varies by even ½ inch (1.3cm), the stone tiles cannot be installed firmly. If there is a spacing problem, it can usually be solved by installing a "sister" joist alongside an existing joist to provide the needed support.

The framing for the curved section here is different from that shown elsewhere in the book but is no less strong. (See the illustration on page 209.) Space the joists correctly, and use blocking to hold them in position. Mark the joist tops for cutting on a curve, and cut each joist carefully, adjusting the saw's bevel for each cut. Install blocking between the joists, at their ends. Then add fascia, which will span between the joists in a curve.

MATERIALS

» **FRAMING FOR BUMP-OUT AREA**
- ❑ 8x8 (20cmx20cm) posts
- ❑ 2x6 (5cmx15cm) cross bracing
- ❑ 2x10 (5cmx25cm) joists and blocking
- ❑ Decking
- ❑ Stone tiles with plastic hardware for installing onto joists

» **RAILING (PAINTED WOOD)**
- ❑ 6x6 (15cmx15cm) posts
- ❑ 1x4s (2.5cmx10cm) for top and bottom sandwich rails
- ❑ 2x2 (5cmx5cm) balusters
- ❑ 2x8 (5cmx20cm) for straight rail cap
- ❑ 2x12 (5cmx30cm) for curved rail cap
- ❑ Post caps

» **OVERHEAD**
- ❑ 6x6 (15cmx15cm) posts
- ❑ 2x8 (5cmx20cm) beam pieces
- ❑ 2x6 (5cmx15cm) rafters (in both directions)

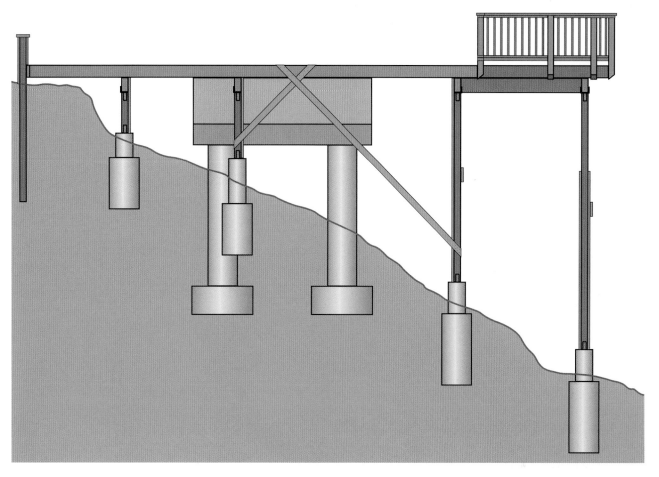

Elevation

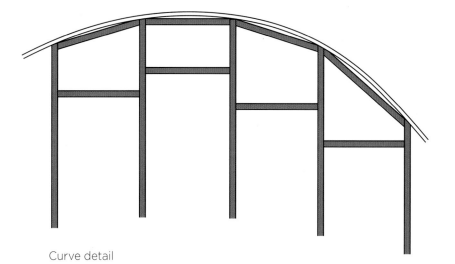

Curve detail

Installing Stone Decking Tiles

Early attempts at making stone or ceramic tiles that one can install over wood framing were unsatisfactory, and tiles regularly cracked or came loose. Newer products perform much better, however, and are reliable and durable if installed correctly.

Recommended decking tiles are made of natural stone, ceramic, or quartzite; they have a firmly adhered composite backing to ensure that they will not crack. You install the tiles using composite connectors called joist plates, which fasten to the deck framing; the tiles then attach to the connectors. (The connection occurs between the composite backing and the connectors; the stone itself is not grabbed.)

Begin the installation using strong 2-by (5cm-by) framing that is framed 16 inches (40.6cm) on center. The framing must be exceptionally square and accurate. Depending on the framing configuration, you may start installing tiles at the deck's edge or somewhere in the middle. Snap chalk lines or stretch a taut mason's line on the tops of joists to ensure that the installation will be perfectly straight. Following manufacturer's instructions, screw down the joist plates, and tap the tiles into the plates using a rubber mallet. The work proceeds in an interlocking pattern, alternating between joist plates and tiles. For extra strength, manufacturers recommend that installers use polyurethane construction adhesive to adhere the tiles on the perimeter.

The tiles are sliced natural stone with a composite backing that interlocks with the joist plates.

This system requires framing made of joists and blocking, all on 12-inch (30.5cm) centers. Take care when installing the blocking pieces, so their top edges are perfectly flush with the joists. As shown here, the blocking is often installed just ahead of the tiles to ensure correct placement.

The joist plates can be simply screwed on top of the framing in most places. However, where the tiles will abut wood decking, use a drill or a grinder to hollow out a space so the plates can be inserted under the decking.

Plates and tiles are installed at the same time, so the plates can be correctly positioned. Make sure the joint lines of the tiles are parallel and consistent in width before fastening the plates.

Tiles often fit tightly into the plates. You may need to tap them into position with a block of wood. Avoid hammering; if you need to use that much force, it's better to reposition a plate or two for an easier fit.

Driving screws into the plates firmly anchors the tiles in place.

Open Nest among the Trees

This big redwood beauty features wide-open spaces, with the elegance of redwood extravagantly displayed. Because of a steep slope, one side is snuggled into the hillside and the other is way up in the air. Multiple trees grow through the floor structure and railings, making the deck feel like a lavish tree house in the forest canopy.

The Design

The homeowners' desire was for an expansive deck, one that would clearly enlarge the house and comfortably handle large gatherings. Incorporating nearby trees was a priority. At the front, the deck had to be elevated more than 20 feet (6.1m); at the back it was actually below ground level.

SHAPE AND SIZE. The triangular upper section at the back, where the entry door is, was prescribed by the hillside; the angled wall pretty much follows the line at which the ground is too high for building. Retaining walls were built, then boxed in with decorative redwood siding; a bench covers the retaining wall where it is low.

Three steps down lead to the capacious main deck, which snakes around the house. To make this as large as possible, the Cloughs cantilevered the deck an unusually long 7 feet (2.1m) past the beam; if you look up at the deck from the underside, it seems to jut out without visible means of support. Installing posts farther out from the house would have detracted from the look of the house.

RAILINGS AND TREES. The through-growing oak trees are a major part of the deck's appeal. The Cloughs framed carefully around the trees so that the decking can be further cut away as they grow and thicken. Even more interestingly, the railings are re-imagined in fanciful ways, to make room for the trunks. The whole arrangement represents a unique affinity with the natural setting.

Fit to the house. As the deck wraps gracefully around the house, the width varies to accommodate the lines of the house.

Easy cleanup. The Cloughs installed the decking with extra-wide gaps between boards to reduce the accumulation of leaves and debris.

Private escape. A corner niche is often a favorite private getaway; here the home's round window, like a piece of art in the background, dresses up the space.

Strategic design. This upper-level triangle-shaped section is lower than the surrounding hill, so a retaining wall, concealed by solid railing and benches, surrounds it.

Unique cutouts. To incorporate a favorite oak tree, the Cloughs neatly cut the decking in several places and lovingly reframed the railing.

Building the Deck

A deck like this is a major construction project. At one end, the hill must be excavated away and a retaining wall built; at the other end, challenging high-elevation work is needed.

FRAMING. The beam in front supports part of the house as well as the deck, so they are built together. The deck joists extend outward 7 feet (2.1m), which is a very long cantilever. A structure like this needs to be carefully engineered. The forward beam is massive, made from 6x14 (15cmx35cm) cedar glue-laminated lumber, which had to be special ordered to fit.

RETAINING WALL, BENCHES, AND RAILINGS. If you have a building area similar to this, a landscaping company should excavate and build retaining walls. Also have them dig the area deep enough so that you can install the beams.

Cover the retaining wall with redwood 2-bys (5cm-bys) of various widths. Here, boards were ripped to create a custom look. Also build benches to cover the retaining wall. Construct standard railings for other parts of the deck.

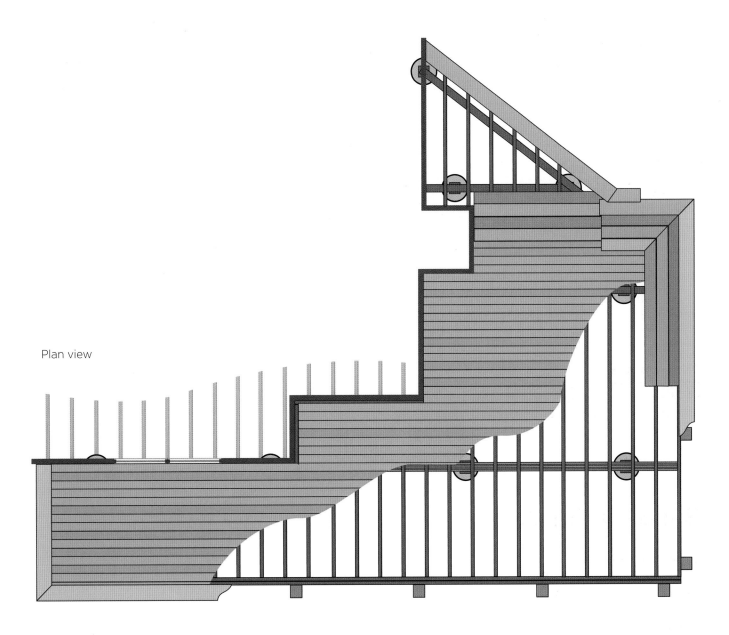

Plan view

MATERIALS

» **FRAMING (ALL TREATED)**
- ❑ 6x6 (15cmx15cm) posts
- ❑ 2x6 (5cmx15cm) cross braces
- ❑ 2x10 (5cmx25cm) joists, ledgers, and headers
- ❑ 6x10 (15cmx25cm) beams
- ❑ 6x14 (15cmx35cm) glue-laminated lumber for large beam
- ❑ Joist hangers
- ❑ 2x10 (5cmx25cm) blocking pieces
- ❑ 2x12 (5cmx30cm) for stair stringers

» **FOOTINGS**
- ❑ Concrete and forms
- ❑ Hardware for posts and beams

» **DECKING AND FASCIA**
- ❑ 2x6 (5cmx15cm) FSC redwood
- ❑ Stainless-steel screws
- ❑ 1-by (2.5cm-by) redwood for fascia

» **RAILING (ALL REDWOOD)**
- ❑ 4x4 (10cmx10cm) posts
- ❑ 2x4 (5cmx10cm) top and bottom rails
- ❑ 2x2 (5cmx5cm) for balusters and rails
- ❑ 2x6 (5cmx15cm) top cap

» **VARIOUS 2-BY (5CM-BY) LUMBER FOR BENCHES AND RETAINING-WALL COVER**

Resource Guide

ALCOA HOME EXTERIORS
201 Isabella St.
Pittsburgh, PA 15212-5858
800-962-6973
www.alcoa.com/alcoahomes
Manufactures aluminum and synthetic
building materials, including deck
products under the Oasis brand.

ANDERSEN CORPORATION
100 Fourth Ave. N.
Bayport, MN 55003-1096
800-426-4261
www.andersenwindows.com
Offers a full line of patio doors
and windows.

**APA – THE ENGINEERED
WOOD ASSOCIATION**
7011 South 19th St.
Tacoma, WA 98466
253-565-6600
www.apawood.org
A nonprofit trade association that
produces a variety of engineered-
wood products.

ARIDDEK
1604 Athens Hwy.
Gainesville, GA 30507
877-270-9387
www.ariddek.com
Manufactures aluminum decking
and railings.

ATLANTIS CABINETRY
3304 Aerial Way Dr.
Roanoke, VA 24018
540-342-0363
www.atlantiscabinetry.com
Manufactures durable, polymer
outdoor cabinetry in a variety of colors
and designs.

AZEK TRIMBOARDS
801 Corey St.
Moosic, PA 18507
877-275-2935
www.azek.com
Makes synthetic trim products, including
balustrades, moldings, and lattice skirting.

BALDWIN LAWN FURNITURE
440 Middlefield St.
Middletown, CT 06457
800-344-5103
www.baldwinfurniture.com
Builds outdoor furniture, planters,
and pergolas.

BLUE RHINO CORPORATION
104 Cambridge Plaza Dr.
Winston-Salem, NC 27104
800-762-1142
www.uniflame.com
Offers a full line of grills, heaters, and
other outdoor appliances, plus a propane
tank exchange program.

**CABLERAIL/FEENEY
ARCHITECTURAL PRODUCTS**
2603 Union St.
Oakland, CA 94607
800-888-2418
www.cablerail.com
Manufactures a line of standard
and custom cable stainless-steel
cable assemblies.

CAL SPAS
1462 East Ninth St.
Pomona, CA 91766
800-225-7727
www.calspas.com
Manufactures barbecue grills, islands,
modular islands, fire pits, and fireplaces
for the outdoors.

**CALIFORNIA REDWOOD
ASSOCIATION**
405 Enfrente Dr., Ste. 200
Novato, CA 94949-7206
888-225-7339
www.calredwood.org
Offers technical information about
the use of redwood for decks and
other structures.

CASCADES
404 Marie-Victorin Blvd.
Kingsey Falls, QC, Canada J0A 1B0
819-363-5100
www.cascades.com
A packaging product leader that also
makes decking from recycled plastic
under the Perma-deck brand.

CECCO TRADING, INC.
600 East Vienna Ave.
Milwaukee, WI 53212
414-445-8989
www.ironwoods.com
Supplies the Iron Wood brand of Ipe
hardwood lumber. Check the Web site to
locate a lumber yard near you.

CLASSIC GARDEN DESIGN
1 Katydid Ln.
Weston, CT
203-226-2886
www.classicgardendesign.com
Designs and installs residential patios,
perennial gardens, pergolas, walks,
fences, and outdoor kitchens.

**CONSUMER PRODUCT SAFETY
COMMISSION (CPSC)**
4330 East West Hwy.
Bethesda, MD 20814
800-638-2772
www.cpsc.gov
Organization charged with protecting the
public from unreasonable risks of serious
injury or death from more than 15,000
types of consumer products.

COOLAROO
P.O. Box 951509
Lake Mary, FL 32795-1509
800-560-4667
www.coolaroo.com
Manufactures shade sails, umbrellas, and
other shade devices that feature knitted
outdoor fabric.

DACOR
1440 Bridge Gate Dr.
Diamond Bar, CA 91765
800-793-0093
www.dacor.com
Designs and manufactures a full line of
outdoor grills, built-in grills, grill carts,
warming ovens, and side burners.

DECKMASTER
205 Mason Cir.
Concord, CA 94520
800-869-1375
www.deckmaster.com
Makes bracket-style hidden
deck fasteners.

DECKORATORS
50 Crestwood Executive Center,
Ste. 308
Crestwood, MO 63126
800-332-5724
www.deckorators.com
Manufactures a wide range of aluminum
balustrades and glass railings in many
colors and designs.

DEKBRANDS
P.O. Box 14804
Minneapolis, MN 55414
800-664-2705
www.deckplans.com
Produces easy-to-do deck systems,
including the award-winning Floating
Foundation Deck System.

DRY-B-LO
475 Tribble Gap Rd., Ste. 305
Cumming, GA 30040
800-437-9256
www.dry-b-lo.com
Manufactures aluminum deck drainage
systems that keep the space below
decks dry.

**EB-TY HIDDEN DECK-FASTENING
SYSTEMS, BLUE HERON
ENTERPRISES, LLC**
P.O. Box 5389
North Branch, NJ 08876
800-438-3289
www.ebty.com
Makes biscuit-style hidden deck fasteners.

**EVERGRAIN COMPOSITE
DECKING, A DIV. OF TAMKO
BUILDING PRODUCTS, INC.**
P.O. Box 1404
Joplin, MO 64802
800-253-1401
www.evergrain.com
Manufactures composite decking
products with realistic, compression-
molded graining patterns.

**FOREST STEWARDSHIP
COUNCIL-U.S.**
1155 30th St. NW, Ste. 300
Washington, D.C. 20007
202-342-0413
www.fscus.org
A nonprofit organization devoted
to encouraging the responsible
management of the world's forests.

GACO WESTERN
P.O. Box 88698
Seattle, WA 98138
866-422-6489
www.gaco.com
Manufactures a high-quality acrylic
polymer waterproof surface protection
for plywood or plank decks.

GALE PACIFIC
P.O. Box 951509
Lake Mary, FL 32795-1509
800-560-4667
www.coolaroo.com
Manufactures a wide range of outdoor
fabrics with various degrees of
UV protection.

GRACE CONSTRUCTION PRODUCTS
62 Whittemore Ave.
Cambridge, MA 02140
800-354-5414
www.graceconstruction.com
www.graceathome.com
Offers self-adhering flashing for decks.

HEARTH & HOME TECHNOLOGIES
20802 Kensington Blvd.
Lakeville, MN 55044
888-669-4328
www.hearthnhome.com
Offers a complete line of gas, electric, and
wood-burning heating products.

HIGHPOINT DECK LIGHTING
P.O. Box 428
Black Hawk, CO 80422
888-582-5850
www.hpdlighting.com
Produces a full line of outdoor lighting,
including railing lights, recessed step
lights, hanging lanterns, wall sconces, and
barbecue cook lights.

HOOKS AND LATTICE
5671 Palmer Way, Ste. K
Carlsbad, CA 92010
800-896-0978
www.hooksandlattice.com
Web site features all styles of window
boxes designed for every application,
including deck railings.

JACUZZI
14525 Monte Vista Ave.
Chino, CA 91710
866-234-7727
www.jacuzzi.com
Manufactures a full line of hot tubs and
deck spas.

LOCKDRY
FSI Home Products Division
2700 Alabama Hwy. 69 S.
Cullman, AL 35057
800-711-1785
www.lockdry.com
Patented aluminum deck and railing
systems with built-in continuous gutters.

MARVIN WINDOWS AND DOORS
P.O. Box 100
Warroad, MN 56763
888-537-7828
www.marvin.com
Makers of windows and doors, including
sliders and French doors.

NANAWALL SYSTEMS, INC.
707 Redwood Hwy.
Mill Valley, CA 94941
800-873-5673
www.nanawall.com
Manufactures folding wall systems of
easy-to-open glass panels.

**NATIONAL FENESTRATION
RATING COUNCIL (NFRC)**
8484 Georgia Ave., Ste. 320
Silver Spring, MD 20910
301-589-1776
www.nfrc.org
A nonprofit organization that administers
the only uniform, independent rating
and labeling system for the energy
performance of patio doors and
other products.

PELLA CORPORATION
102 Main St.
Pella, IA 50219
800-374-4758
www.pella.com
Produces energy-efficient patio doors
and windows.

**PENN DUTCH STRUCTURES AT
THE MARKETS AT SHREWSBURY**
12025 Susquehanna Trail
Glen Rock, PA 17327

PROCELL DECKING SYSTEMS
11746 Foley Beach Express
Foley, AL 36535
251-943-2916
www.procelldeck.com
Manufactures synthetic decking from
PVC that's stain and scratch resistant.

PROGRESS LIGHTING
P.O. Box 5704
Spartanburg, SC 29304-5704
864-599-6000
www.progresslighting.com
Makes wall lanterns that have motion
detectors built into the mounting plate
or the lantern itself, as well as deck and
landscape lights.

PUNCH! SOFTWARE, LLC
7900 NW 100th St., Ste. LL6
Kansas City, MO 64153
800-365-4832
www.punchsoftware.com
Software company specializing in home
and landscaping design programs.

ROYAL CROWN LIMITED
P.O. Box 360
Milford, IN 46542-0360
800-488-5245
www.royalcrownltd.com
Produces vinyl deck planks and railing
products under the Triple Crown Fence,
Brock Deck Systems, Brock Deck, and
Deck Lok Systems brands.

SHADE SAILS LLC
7028 Greenleaf Ave., Ste. K
Whittier, CA 90602
562-945-9952
www.shadesails.com
Imports tensioned, UV-treated
fabric canopies.

SHADESCAPES USA
39300 Back River Rd.
Paonia, CO 81428
866-997-4233
www.shadescapesusa.com
Manufactures side- and center-post
shade umbrellas.

SOUTHERN PINE COUNCIL
2900 Indiana Ave.
Kenner, LA 70065-4605
504-443-4464
www.southernpine.com
A trade association that offers
information on deck building with
treated lumber.

STARBORN INDUSTRIES, INC.
27 Engelhard Ave.
Avenel, NJ 07001
800-596-7747
www.starbornindustries.com
Manufactures stainless-steel deck
fastening systems, including Headcote
and DeckFast brand screws.

SUMMER CLASSICS
P.O. Box 390
7000 Hwy. 25
Montevallo, AL 35115
205-987-3100
www.summerclassics.com
Manufactures deck and garden
furnishings in wrought aluminum,
wrought iron, and woven resin.

SUMMERWOOD PRODUCTS
735 Progress Ave.
Toronto, ON, Canada M1H 2W7
866-519-4634
www.summerwood.com
Offers prefab customized kits for
outdoor structures such as gazebos, pool
cabanas, and spa enclosures.

SUNDANCE SPAS
14525 Monte Vista Ave.
Chino, CA 91710
800-883-7727
www.sundancespas.com
The largest manufacturer of acrylic spas.

**SUSTAINABLE FORESTRY
INITIATIVE, A DIV. OF AMERICAN
FOREST & PAPER ASSOCIATION**
1111 Nineteenth St. NW, Ste. 800
Washington, D.C. 20036
www.aboutsfi.org
A comprehensive forestry management
program developed by the American
Forest & Paper Association.

**TAMKO BUILDING PRODUCTS,
INC. EVERGRAIN COMPOSITE
DECKING ELEMENTS DECKING**
220 West 4th St.
Joplin, MO 64801
800-641-4691
www.tamko.com
www.evergrain.com
www.elementsdecking.com
Manufactures composite decking
products using compression molding
for a real wood look. Visit the Web site
for a photo gallery and distributors in
your area.

TIGER CLAW INC.
400 Middle St., Ste. J
Bristol, CT 06010-8405
800-928-4437
www.deckfastener.com
Manufactures products for the
construction industry, including hidden
deck fasteners.

TIMBERTECH
894 Prairie Ave.
Wilmington, OH 45177
800-307-7780
www.timbertech.com
Manufacturers composite decking
and railing systems, fascia boards, and
specialty trim.

TIMBER TREATMENT TECHNOLOGIES
8700 Trail Lake Dr., Ste. 101
Germantown, TN 38125
866-318-9432
www.timbersil.com
Developer of a new process for preserving wood. The formula, nontoxic and noncorrosive, is designed for both aboveground and in-ground applications.

TREX COMPANY, INC.
160 Exeter Dr.
Winchester, VA 22603
800-289-8739
www.trex.com
Specializes in composite decking materials.

UNIVERSAL FOREST PRODUCTS, INC.
2801 East Beltline Ave. NE
Grand Rapids, MI 49525
616-364-6161
www.ufpi.com
Manufactures and distributes wood and wood-alternative products for decking and railing systems. Also manufactures Veranda brand products.

WESTERN RED CEDAR LUMBER ASSOCIATION (WRCLA)
1501-700 W. Pender St.
Pender Place 1, Business Building
Vancouver, BC, Canada V6C 1G8
866-778-9096
www.realcedar.org
www.wrcla.org
www.cedar-deck.org
A nonprofit trade association representing quality producers of western red cedar in the U.S. and Canada. Its Web site explains how to select appropriate grades.

WEYERHAEUSER CO.
P.O. Box 1237
Springdale, AR 72765
800-951-5117
www.choicedek.com
Offers ChoiceDek brand decking manufactured from a blend of low- and high-density polyethylene plastic and wood fibers. Also distributes CedarOne cedar decking.

WOLMAN WOOD CARE PRODUCTS, A DIV. OF ZINSSER CO., INC.
173 Belmont Dr.
Somerset, NJ 08875
800-556-7737
www.wolman.com
Makes products used to restore, beautify, and protect decks and other exterior wood structures.

Photo Credits

ALL PHOTOS BY STEVE CORY UNLESS OTHERWISE NOTED.

page 1: Flat Rock Photography **page 4:** *top* Joel Boyer; *bottom* Flat Rock Photography **page 5:** *top* Clough Construction; *second from top* Joel Boyer **page 8:** Joel Boyer **page 9:** Clemens Jellema **page 11:** Clough Construction **page 12:** Flat Rock Photography **page 13:** *top* Clough Construction **page 14:** *left* Clemens Jellema **page 15:** *bottom* Clough Construction **page 17:** *top* Flat Rock Photography; *bottom* Joel Boyer **page 18:** *left* Flat Rock Photography **page 20:** Clemens Jellema **page 21:** *top* Flat Rock Photography; *bottom* Clemens Jellema **page 24:** *top* Gustavo de la Cruz **page 27:** *all* courtesy of California Redwood Association **page 29:** *all* Flat Rock Photography **page 30:** Joel Boyer **page 32:** *bottom* Flat Rock Photography **pages 32–33:** Clough Construction **page 35:** Joel Boyer **page 37:** *top right* Joel Boyer **page 67:** Clemens Jellema **page 68:** Clemens Jellema **page 69:** *top* Clemens Jellema **page 70:** Clemens Jellema **page 76:** *right* Clemens Jellema **page 77:** *top* Clemens Jellema **pages 80-82:** Clemens Jellema **page 89:** *top* Clemens Jellema **pages 92–103:** Clemens Jellema **pages 122–123:** Trex Company, Inc. **page 130:** *left* Gustavo de la Cruz; *right* Trex Company, Inc. **page 131:** *top left* Trex Company, Inc.; *top right, bottom left, and bottom right* Kim Katwijk **pages 146–179:** Flat Rock Photography **page 182:** Trevor Henley, Henley Photography **page 183:** Clough Construction **page 185:** *top, and bottom right* Clough Construction **page 186:** *bottom right* Clough Construction **page 187:** *top left, top right, and bottom left* Clough Construction **page 196:** *top* Trevor Henley, Henley Photography; *bottom* Clough Construction **page 197:** *top right* Trevor Henley, Henley Photography; *bottom* Clough Construction **page 212:** *top* Trevor Henley, Henley Photography **page 213:** Trevor Henley, Henley Photography **page 214:** *left and right* Clough Construction; *center* Trevor Henley, Henley Photography

Glossary

ACTUAL DIMENSIONS: The exact measurements of a piece of lumber after it has been cut, surfaced, and dried. For example, a 2x4's (5cmx10cm) actual dimensions are 1½ x 3½ inches (3.8cmx8.9cm).

BALUSTERS: The numerous vertical pieces, often made of 2x2s (5cmx5cm) or 1x4s (2.5cmx10cm), that fill in spaces between rails and provide a fence-like structure.

BAND JOIST: Any joist that defines the perimeter of a deck, including the header joist and end, or outside, joists. Also called rim joist.

BEAM: A large framing member, usually four-by (10cm-by) material or doubled-up two-bys (5cm-bys), which is attached horizontally to the posts and used to support joists.

BLOCKING: Usually solid pieces of lumber the same dimensions as the joists, which are cut to fit snugly between the joists to prevent excessive warping. Also called bridging or bracing.

BUILDING CODES: Municipal rules regulating safe building practices and procedures. Generally, the codes encompass structural, electrical, plumbing, and mechanical remodeling and new construction. Confirmation of conformity to local codes by inspection may be required.

BUILDING PERMIT: A license that authorizes permission to do work on your home. Minor repairs and remodeling work usually do not call for a permit, but if the job consists of extending the water supply and drain, waste, vent system; adding an electrical circuit; or making structural changes to a building, a building permit may be necessary.

CANTILEVER: Construction that extends beyond its vertical support.

CURING: The slow chemical action that hardens concrete.

DECKING: Boards nailed to joists to form the deck surface.

ELEVATION: Architectural drawing of a structure seen from the side, rear, or front view.

FASCIA BOARD: Facing that covers the exposed ends and sides of decking to provide a finished appearance.

FOOTING: The concrete base that supports posts or steps.

FROST LINE: The maximum depth to which soil freezes. The local building department can provide information on the frost-line depth in your area.

GRADE: The ground level. On-grade means at or on the natural ground level.

HEADER JOIST: Band joist attached and running at a right angle to common joists, enabling them to maintain correct spacing and stiffening their ends.

JOIST: Structural member, usually two-by (5cm-by) lumber, commonly placed perpendicularly across beams to support deck boards.

JOIST HANGER: Metal connector used to join a joist and beam so that the tops are in the same plane.

KNOT: The high-density root of a limb that is very dense but is not connected to the surrounding wood.

LAG SCREW: Large wood screw (usually ¼ inch (0.6cm) or more in diameter) with a bolt-like hex head usually used to attached ledgers to house framing. Often incorrectly called lag bolt.

LATTICE: A cross-pattern structure that is made of wood, metal, or plastic.

LEDGER: Horizontal board attached to the side of a house or wall to support a deck or an overhead cover.

NOMINAL DIMENSIONS: The identifying dimensions of a piece of lumber [e.g., 2x4 (5cmx10cm)] which are larger than the actual dimensions [1½x3½ (3.8cmx8.9cm)].

PENNY (ABBREVIATED "D") Unit of measurement for nail length; e.g., a 10d nail is 3 inches (7.6cm) long.

PERMANENT STRUCTURE: Any structure that is anchored to the ground or a house.

PLAN DRAWING: A drawing that gives an overhead view of the deck showing where all footings and lumber pieces go.

PLUMB: Vertically straight, in relation to a horizontally level surface.

PLUNGE CUT: A cut that can't begin from the outside of the board and must be made from the middle.

POST: A vertical member, usually 4x4 (10cmx10cm) or 6x6 (15cmx15cm), that supports either the deck or railing.

POST ANCHOR: A metal fastener designed to keep the post from wandering and to inhibit rot by holding the post a bit above the concrete.

POSTHOLE DIGGER: A clamshell-type tool used to dig holes for posts.

POWER AUGER: A tool that is powered by a gasoline engine and used for drilling into the ground. Often used in larger projects to dig postholes.

PRESSURE-TREATED LUMBER: Wood that has had preservatives forced into it under pressure to make it repel rot and insects.

ON CENTER: A point of reference for measuring. For example, "16 inches (40.6cm) on center" means 16 inches (40.6cm) from the center of one framing member to the center of the next.

RABBET: A ledge cut along one edge of a workpiece.

RAIL: A horizontal member that is placed between posts and used for support or as a barrier.

RAILING: Assembly made from balusters attached to rails and installed between posts as a safety barrier at the edge of a deck.

RAILING CAP: A horizontal piece of lumber laid flat on top of a post and top rail, covering the end grain of the post and providing a flat surface wide enough to set objects on.

RECOMMENDED SPAN: The distance a piece of lumber can safely traverse without being supported underneath.

REDWOOD: A straight-grain, weather-resistant wood used for outdoor building.

RIM JOIST: See Band joist.

RIP CUT: A cut made with the grain on a piece of wood.

RISER: Vertical boards placed between stringers on stairs to support stair treads. They are optional on exterior stairs.

SITE PLAN: A drawing that maps out your house and yard. Also called a base plan.

SKEWING: Driving two nails at opposing angles. This technique creates a sounder connection by "hooking" the boards together as well as by reducing the possibility of splitting.

SKIRT: Solid band of horizontal wood members (fascia) installed around the deck perimeter to conceal exposed ends of joists and deck boards.

STRINGER: On stairs, the diagonal boards that support the treads and risers; also called a stair horse.

TACK-NAIL: To nail one structural member to another temporarily with a minimal amount of nails.

TOENAIL: Joining two boards together by nailing at an angle through the end, or toe, on one board and into the face of another.

TREAD: On stairs, the horizontal boards supported by the stringers.

Metric Equivalents

LENGTH

1 inch	25.4 mm
1 foot	0.3048 m
1 yard	0.9144 m
1 mile	1.61 km

AREA

1 square inch	645 mm^2
1 square foot	0.0929 m^2
1 square yard	0.8361 m^2
1 acre	4046.86 m^2
1 square mile	2.59 km^2

VOLUME

1 cubic inch	16.3870 cm^3
1 cubic foot	0.03 m^3
1 cubic yard	0.77 m^3

COMMON LUMBER EQUIVALENTS

Sizes: Metric cross sections are so close to their U.S. sizes, as noted below, that for most purposes they may be considered equivalents.

Dimensional lumber

1 x 2	19 x 38 mm
1 x 4	19 x 89 mm
2 x 2	38 x 38 mm
2 x 4	38 x 89 mm
2 x 6	38 x 140 mm
2 x 8	38 x 184 mm
2 x 10	38 x 235 mm
2 x 12	38 x 286 mm

Sheet sizes

4 x 8 ft.	1200 x 2400 mm
4 x 10 ft.	1200 x 3000 mm

Sheet thicknesses

¼ in.	6 mm
⅜ in.	9 mm
½ in.	12 mm
¾ in.	19 mm

Stud/joist spacing

16 in. o.c.	400 mm o.c.
24 in. o.c.	600 mm o.c.

CAPACITY

1 fluid ounce	29.57 mL
1 pint	473.18 mL
1 quart	1.14 L
1 gallon	3.79 L

WEIGHT

1 ounce	28.35g
1 pound	0.45kg

TEMPERATURE

Fahrenheit = Celsius x 1.8 + 32
Celsius = Fahrenheit − 32 x 5⁄9

NAIL SIZE & LENGTH

Penny Size	Nail Length
2d	1"
3d	1¼"
4d	1½"
5d	1¾"
6d	2"
7d	2¼"
8d	2½"
9d	2¾"
10d	3"
12d	3¼"
16d	3½"

Index

A

Amish Pavilion, 102–3
Arana, Ivan (Decks, Inc.)
  about, 30, 31, 66–73
    contact information, 66
    craftsmanship, 71
    design approach, 68
    finish materials, 68
    making it dry under deck, 92–93
    techniques, 72, 80–85
  featured projects
    Amish Pavilion, 102–3
    Beautiful Symmetry, 94–97
    Expansive Balcony, 86–91
    Well Rounded, 74–79
    Woodsy Retreat, 98–101
    Woody Gem, 104–7

B

balcony, expansive, 86–89
balusters
  designing, 15
  example photos, 15
  materials options, 15
  railing structure and, 24
  types of, illustrated, 158–59. See also
    projects, featured
Barrett Outdoors. See de la Cruz, Gustavo
beams, 23, 24
benches
  designing decks and, 15, 16
  planters with, 69, 82
  projects with, 40–45, 70–79, 94–97,
    166–69, 176–81, 212–15
  serving multiple purposes, 8, 42, 56
  "Z"-shaped, 14
bending decking and railing, 130–31
book overview, 8–9
Boyer, Joel (Unique Deck Builders)
  about, 30, 34–41
    contact information, 34
    design approach, 36–37
    finish materials, 37
    techniques, 38
  featured projects
    Cozy Retreat, 46–51
    Private City Loft, 60–65
    Spacious Rooftop Getaway, 52–55
    Split-Level with Wood Bar and Spa,
      40–45
    Versatile Family Room, 56–59
bridging (blocking), 23
builders, about, 30. See also specific
  builder names

C

cedar, 28
ceilings. See pergolas; roofs
city, featured projects in. See Boyer, Joel
  (Unique Deck Builders)
Clough, Deanne and Scott (Clough
  Construction)
  about, 30, 32, 182–89

contact information, 182
  design approaches, 184–86
  engineering for strength, 186
  materials used, 184, 196–97
  sustainability focus, 186
  techniques, 188
featured projects
  Movie Star Setting, 204–9
  Natural Jewel, 190–95
  Open Nest Among the Trees, 212–15
  Sunset Setting, 198–203
code, meeting, 26
color, designing palette, 13, 14
composite material
  about, 28
  bending, 130–31
  design considerations, 13, 184
  featured projects, 198–203. See also
    Arana, Ivan; de la Cruz, Gustavo;
    Streett, Barry
  sustainability and, 186
cooking areas, 18. See also grills and
  grilling areas; kitchens, outdoor
cost per square foot, 34, 71
counters. See kitchens, outdoor
curves, 151

D

de la Cruz, Gustavo "Gus" (Barrett
  Outdoors)
  about, 30, 32, 108–15
    bending decking and railing, 130–31
    contact information, 108
    decking and railing materials, 113
    designing around furniture, 110
    designs that pop, 110
    metal framing, 122–23
    outdoor kitchens and lighting, 113
    techniques, 114
  featured projects
    Curvy Party Deck, 124–29
    Half Circle with Wings, 142–45
    Jewel by the Pool, 116–21
    Relaxation Station, 132–35
    Zigzag Charm, 136–41
decking boards
  angled, 25
  fancy design ideas, 80–81
  structure of deck and, 24
  types of materials, 28
decking tiles, stone, 204–11
decks
  appeal, benefits of, 6
  designing. See designing decks
  family activities and, 7, 10, 12
  keeping dry under, 92–93
  protecting, 26
  structure of, 23–26
Decks, Inc.. See Arana, Ivan
designing decks, 10–29
  color, 13, 14
  details, 16
  focal points, 14

guidelines for, 10
  height, 14
  home style and, 16
  outdoor rooms, 18–19
  porch option, 21, 70
  shape, 12
  size, 12
  theme, 14
  visual considerations, 13–16
  weather considerations, 17
designs. See projects, featured
details, design ideas, 16
dining areas. See also kitchens, outdoor
  design ideas, 18, 20, 43, 47, 71, 111, 112
  designing around furniture, 110
  projects with, 52–65, 74–79, 86–89,
    104–7, 116–21, 124–29, 136–45, 160–81,
    190–95, 204–9

F

family activities, 7, 10, 12
family rooms, 56–59, 170–75
fans, ceiling, 63, 89, 127, 128, 172, 173, 174
fascia, 15, 23, 24, 28, 85. See also specific
  projects
featured projects. See projects, featured;
  specific designers
fire pits, 14, 98, 99, 124, 125, 126, 132, 143,
  166, 170, 172
fireplaces, 148, 154, 156
flashing, 24
focal points, 14
footings. See piers (footings)
framing. See structure of deck
furniture, designing around, 110

G

gardening, 22. See also landscape
girders, 23
grills and grilling areas. See also kitchens,
  outdoor
  built-in grills, 51, 113, 117, 178
  design ideas, 19, 20, 41, 46, 47, 53, 118,
    142, 173
  out-of-the-way, 87, 96, 137

H

height, planning/designing, 14
hot tubs. See spas or hot tubs

I

ironwoods, 28

J

joist hardware, 25
joists, 23, 24

K

kitchens, outdoor. See also grills and
  grilling areas
  below deck, 92
  counter ideas, 50–51, 56, 57, 58, 111, 127,
    155, 156

design considerations, 19, 36, 148, 184
lighting and, 22, 113
projects with, 116–29, 142–45, 154–57, 170–81
under shade tree, 186

L

landscape. *See also* planters
design guidelines, 15, 17
gardening, 22
lattice
roofing, 17
skirting, 43, 44, 47, 94–95, 133
trellis walls/fences, 17, 21, 37, 52, 54–55, 62, 63, 65, 197
ledger, 24, 26
lighting
ceiling, 113, 126, 127, 128, 172, 173
low-voltage, 22, 77
options, 22
photos of, 22, 77, 83, 89, 92, 100, 105, 106, 159, 172, 173
post, 83, 89, 105, 106, 156, 159
railing, 78, 100
sconces, 53, 89
step, 77
living rooms, outdoor, 20–21, 53, 62, 125, 136, 154, 156, 170–71, 201
loft, private city, 60–65
lounging areas, 18, 36, 42, 52, 53, 56, 75, 104, 149, 161, 167

M

materials. *See also* decking boards
bending composite material, 130–31
budget and, 25
projects illustrating types/uses. *See* projects, featured
sizing, 26
structural, 27
structure of deck and, 23–26
visible, 28–29
wood species and grading, 27
metal framing, 122–23

O

outdoor rooms, 18–19. *See also* dining areas; family rooms; kitchens, outdoor; living rooms, outdoor

P

paths, 19
pergolas
benefits of, 17, 21
example photos/designs, 14, 47, 48–49, 53, 62, 64, 68, 88, 90, 149, 197
lattice panels on, 17, 53
plants on, 22
piers (footings), 23, 26
planters
benches with, 69, 82
design ideas, 15, 16, 22

projects with, 176–81
plugging/sinking fasteners, 85
porches, 21, 70, 148, 166
posts
lights. *See* lighting
notched support, 25
railing, 24, 83
for stairs, 84
structural, 23, 25
projects, featured
Amish Pavilion, 102–3
Beautiful Symmetry, 94–97
Cozy Retreat, 46–51
Curved This Way, Then That, 160–63
Curvy Party Deck, 124–29
by designer. *See specific designers*
Expansive Balcony, 86–91
Half Circle with Wings, 142–45
Jewel by the Pool, 116–21
Log Cabin Chic, 154–57
Movie Star Setting, 204–9
Natural Jewel, 190–95
Open Nest Among the Trees, 212–15
Private City Loft, 60–65
Private Family Room, 170–75
Relaxation Station, 132–35
Rocky Mountain High Life, 176–81
Scallops and Curves, 164–69
Spacious Rooftop Getaway, 52–55
Split-Level with Wood Bar and Spa, 40–45
Sunset Setting, 198–203
Versatile Family Room, 56–59
Well Rounded, 74–79
Woodsy Retreat, 98–101
Woody Gem, 104–7
Zigzag Charm, 136–41
protecting deck, 26, 27

R

railing
attaching, 84
curves and, 130–31, 151
design guidelines, 15
plugging/sinking fasteners, 85
posts, 24, 83
structure of, 24
types of, illustrated, 158–59. *See also* projects, featured
view and, 15
redwood, 28, 196–97. *See also* Clough, Deanne and Scott (Clough Construction)
Rolling Ridge Deck and Outdoor Living. *See* Streett, Barry
roofs. *See also* pergolas
design considerations, 17
example photos/designs, 21, 170, 171, 173
fireplace/outdoor kitchen, 156
gable, with flying rafters, 124, 126, 128–29
pavilion, 100, 101, 102–3

with pillars, 117, 120, 121
rooftop decks, 37, 38, 52–55, 211

S

shape of deck, designing, 12
size of deck, designing, 12
skylights, 21, 173, 174
spas or hot tubs
design ideas, 19, 149, 185, 187
projects with, 40–45, 74–79, 98–101, 160–63, 170–75
slab for, 78
stairs
box framing for, 82
cascading, 36
curved/curving, 118, 148, 167
design considerations, 12, 36, 68, 74–79
projects with, 40–65, 116–21, 124–29, 133–45, 154–57, 160–80, 190–95, 198–203
railing posts, 84
spiral, 29
structure/components of, 24
stone decking tiles, 204–11
Streett, Barry (Rolling Ridge Deck and Outdoor Living)
about, 30, 32, 146–53
contact information, 146
design process, 148
kitchens and fireplaces, 148
railing types, illustrated, 158–59
railings and curves, 151
techniques, 152
featured projects
Curved This Way, Then That, 160–63
Log Cabin Chic, 154–57
Private Family Room, 170–75
Rocky Mountain High Life, 176–81
Scallops and Curves, 164–69
structure of deck, 23–26, 122–23, 186
sunning areas, 18. *See also* lounging areas
sustainability, 186
symmetrical deck, 94–97
synthetics. *See* composite material

T

theme, designing, 14
trellis walls, 21, 37, 52, 54–55, 62, 63, 64, 65, 197, 206

U

Unique Deck Builders. *See* Boyer, Joel

V

views, optimizing, 15

W

water, keeping from under deck, 92–93
weather considerations, 17
wood. *See* materials

Safety

Although the methods in this book have been reviewed for safety, it is not possible to overstate the importance of using the safest methods you can. What follows are reminders—some do's and don'ts of work safety—to use along with your common sense.

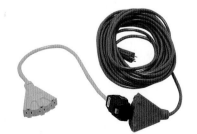

■ Always use caution, care, and good judgment when following the procedures described in this book.

■ Always be sure that the electrical setup is safe, that no circuit is overloaded, and that all power tools and outlets are properly grounded. Do not use power tools in wet locations.

■ Always read container labels on paints, solvents, and other products; provide ventilation; and observe all other warnings.

■ Always read the manufacturer's instructions for using a tool, especially the warnings.

■ Use hold-downs and push sticks whenever possible when working on a table saw. Avoid working short pieces if you can.

■ Always remove the key from any drill chuck (portable or press) before starting the drill.

■ Always pay deliberate attention to how a tool works so that you can avoid being injured.

■ Always know the limitations of your tools. Do not try to force them to do what they were not designed to do.

■ Always make sure that any adjustment is locked before proceeding. For example, always check the rip fence on a table saw or the bevel adjustment on a portable saw before starting to work.

■ Always clamp small pieces to a bench or other work surface when using a power tool.

■ Always wear the appropriate rubber gloves or work gloves when handling chemicals, moving or stacking lumber, working with concrete, or doing heavy construction.

■ Always wear a disposable face mask when you create dust by sawing or sanding. Use a special filtering respirator when working with toxic substances and solvents.

■ Always wear eye protection, especially when using power tools or striking metal on metal or concrete; a chip can fly off, for example, when chiseling concrete.

■ Never work while wearing loose clothing, open cuffs, or jewelry; tie back long hair.

■ Always be aware that there is seldom enough time for your body's reflexes to save you from injury from a power tool in a dangerous situation; everything happens too fast. Be alert!

■ Always keep your hands away from the business ends of blades, cutters, and bits.

■ Always hold a circular saw firmly, usually with both hands.

■ Always use a drill with an auxiliary handle to control the torque when using large-size bits.

■ Always check your local building codes when planning new construction. The codes are intended to protect public safety and should be observed to the letter.

■ Never work with power tools when you are tired or when under the influence of alcohol or drugs.

■ Never cut tiny pieces of wood or pipe using a power saw. When you need a small piece, saw it from a securely clamped longer piece.

■ Never change a saw blade or a drill or router bit unless the power cord is unplugged. Do not depend on the switch being off. You might accidentally hit it.

■ Never work in insufficient lighting.

■ Never work with dull tools. Have them sharpened, or learn how to sharpen them yourself.

■ Never use a power tool on a workpiece—large or small—that is not firmly supported.

■ Never saw a workpiece that spans a large distance between horses without close support on each side of the cut; the piece can bend, closing on and jamming the blade, causing saw kickback.

■ When sawing, never support a workpiece from underneath with your leg or other part of your body.

■ Never carry sharp or pointed tools, such as utility knives, awls, or chisels, in your pocket. If you want to carry any of these tools, use a special-purpose tool belt that has leather pockets and holders.